NINJA
AIR FRYER
COOKBOOK

#2021

Amazingly Easy, Crispy & Healthy Recipes That Any Fried Favorites Can Cook

BY

Dr. Paula Coleman

Table of Contents

INTRODUCTION

Meaning of Ninja Air Fryer Max XL

The Ninja Air Fryer is a low-fat, healthier way to cook your favorite fried foods from fluffy, golden chips and crispy chicken wings to roasted vegetables, enjoy the same great taste using little to no oil. With Ninja air fryers, you can make all the crispy, fried meals and snacks you crave without the guilt. Air fryer ovens are the greaseless fryer option when it comes to cooking fried foods.

It offers a quick and easy way to cook meals and snacks - from perfectly cooked chips and crispy chicken wings to delicate fish and golden vegetables using little to no oil. Up to 75% less fat than traditional frying methods.

Not only can you create delicious mains and side dishes with the air fryer, you can also reheat leftovers to retain the taste and texture – perfect for pizza. You can even gently dehydrate ingredients to enjoy dried fruit and herbs, vegetable crisps and homemade beef jerky. It can cook from frozen for deliciously crispy results, without the need to defrost food first. When compared to deep fried, hand-cut French Fries, the Ninja Air Fryer gives you the same great taste but uses little to no oil.

About the Ninja Air Fryer Max XL

Guilt-free fried food using little to no oil.

Lower fat alternative to traditional frying methods.

Four cooking functions – Air Fry, Roast, Reheat and Dehydrate.

Air Fry – Up to 75 Percent less fat than traditional frying methods.

Dishwasher-safe parts. Includes 3. 8 L non-stick basket with crisper plate.

How the Ninja Air Fryer Max XL Works

The Ninja Air Fryer Max XL has an enhanced control panel of multiple preset programs such as max crisp, air fry, air roast, air broil, bake, reheat and dehydrate; in addition to up and down buttons for temp and time. Each preset program per Ninja is set to have optimized fan speeds for better results.

It makes use of Max Crisp Technology that enables it to cook foods up to 30% faster than other Ninja AF100 series. With the air fryer cooker at home, no more salt and fat laden food to clog up your arteries!

Getting to Know Your Ninja Air Fryer Max XL

Function Buttons:

- **Max Crisp:** It can be used for frozen foods to give them extra crispiness and crunch with little to no oil.
- **Air Fry:** It is used give food crispiness and crunch with little to no oil.
- **Air Roast:** It can be used to roast certain foods like tender meats, vegetables, and more.
- **Air Broil:** Use to caramelize and brown food.
- **Bake:** It can be used for baking treats and desserts.
- **Reheat:** It can be used warming leftovers to give you crispy results.
- **Dehydrate:** Dehydrate meats, fruits, and vegetables for healthy snacks.

Operating Buttons:

- **TEMP arrows:** The up and down TEMP arrows can be used to adjust the cook temperature in any function, except Max Crisp, before or during cooking.
- **TIME arrows:** The up and down TIME arrows to adjust the cook time in any function before or during cooking.
- **START/STOP button:** The button can be used to start cooking after selecting the time and temperature. You can stop cooking at any time by pressing the button again.
- **POWER button:** This button can be used to shuts off the unit and stops all cooking modes.

NOTE: The unit can enter standby mode where's no activity with the control panel after 10 minutes. The Power button will be dimly lit.

Using the Cooking Buttons

To turn on the unit, first plug the power cord into a wall outlet. Press the power button.

1. **Air Fry:**
    *   Place the crisper plate in the basket.
    *   Select the AIR FRY function. The default temperature setting will display. Use the TEMP up and down arrow buttons to set your preferred temperature.
    *   Press the TIME up and down arrow function to set the cook time.

NOTE: Always allow the air fryer to preheat for about 3 minutes 3 minutes before adding ingredients to produce good results.

*   Place the ingredients to the air fryer basket. Transfer the basket in the unit.
*   Press START/STOP to start cooking.
*   To toss ingredients halfway during the cooking process, remove basket and shake it back and forth. The unit will automatically pause when the basket is removed. Add the basket into the unit and cooking will resume.
*   Once the cooking cycle is done, the unit will beep and End will appear on the control panel display.
*   Transfer the ingredients by dumping them out or silicone-tipped tongs/utensils.

2. **Max Crisp:**
    *   Place the crisper plate in the basket.
    *   Click the MAX CRISP button. The default temperature setting will display. The temperature of the Max Crisp button cannot be adjusted.
    *   Select the TIME up and down arrow buttons to set the cook time.
    *   Add ingredients to the basket. Insert the basket in the unit.
    *   Press START/STOP to begin cooking.
    *   To toss ingredients during cooking, remove basket and shake it back and forth. The unit will automatically pause when the basket is removed. Reinsert basket and cooking will resume.
    *   Once the cooking cycle is done, the unit will beep and End will appear on the control panel display.
    *   Remove ingredients by dumping them out or silicone tipped tongs/utensils.

3. **Bake:**
    *   Place the crisper plate or baking dish in the basket.
    *   Click the BAKE button. The default temperature setting will display. Press the TEMP up and down arrow buttons to set your desired temperature.
    *   Press the TIME up and down arrow buttons to set the cook time.
    *   Add ingredients to the basket. Insert the basket in the unit.
    *   Click START/STOP to begin cooking.
    *   When cooking is complete, the unit will beep and End will appear on the control panel display.

- Remove ingredients by dumping them out or silicone-tipped tongs/utensils.

4. **Air Roast:**
- Place the crisper plate in the basket.
- Click the AIR ROAST button. The default temperature setting will display. Press the TEMP up and down arrow buttons to set your desired temperature.
- Press the TIME up and down arrow buttons to set the cook time.
- Add ingredients to the basket. Insert the basket in the unit.
- Press START/STOP to begin cooking.
- When cooking is complete, the unit will beep and End will appear on the control panel display.
- Remove ingredients by dumping them out or silicone-tipped tongs/utensils.

5. **Dehydrate:**
- Add a layer of ingredients in the air fryer basket. Place crisper plate in the basket and set a second layer of ingredients on the crisper plate.
- Transfer the basket in the unit.
- Click the DEHYDRATE button. The default temperature will display. Use the TEMP up and down arrow buttons to set your desired temperature.
- Click the TIME up and down arrow buttons to set the dehydrating time.
- Press START/STOP to start dehydrating.
- When dehydrating is complete, the unit will beep and END will appear on the control panel display.

6. **Air Broil:**

NOTE: The Air Broil function and broil rack are not included on all Ninja Air Fryer models.

- Place the crisper plate and broil rack in the air fryer basket.
- Click the AIR BROIL button. The default temperature setting will display. Use the TEMP up and down arrow buttons to set your desired temperature.
- Press the TIME up and down arrow buttons to set the cook time.
- Add ingredients to the basket. Transfer the basket in the unit.
- Click START/STOP to begin cooking.
- When cooking is complete, the unit will beep and End will appear on the control panel display.
- Remove ingredients by dumping them out or silicone tipped tongs/utensils.

7. **Reheat:**
- Place the crisper plate in the basket.
- Click the REHEAT button. The default temperature setting will display. Press the TEMP up and down arrow buttons to set your desired temperature.
- Press the TIME up and down arrow buttons to set the reheating time.
- Add ingredients to the basket. Insert the basket in the unit.
- Press START/STOP to begin reheating.

- When reheating is complete, the unit will beep and End will appear on the control panel display.
- Remove ingredients by dumping them out or using oven mitts or silicone tipped tongs/utensils.

Benefits of Using Ninja Air Fryer Max XL

1. **Fuss-Free Air Fryer:**

The air fryer is very simple and easy to use with few buttons to press. All you've to do is to set the timer as well as the temperature and the meal is ready when the timer goes off.

2. **Novice Can Cook:**

A complete novice with no prior knowledge of cooking can whip up delicious meals with the air frying machine for home use. You just have to select the accurate cooking time and temperature according to the taste and texture you desire. All the hard magic is done inside the air fryer.

3. **No Oily Mess to Clean Up:**

The air fryer has a cover that allows all the cooking process to be carried out inside the machine. Its great than deep frying with a frying pan or skillet with an exposed cooking surface. No oily mess up to clean apart from the removable air fryer basket, drip pan or cooking bowl.

4. **Saves on Cooking Oil:**

Oil is not required in cooking with the air fryer, so you get to save on oil. The air fryer only requires few tablespoons of oil required for air frying to turn out crispy.

5. **Easy to Clean:**

The air fryer is very easy to clean and all the removable parts are dishwater safe. When the dishwater is unavailable, soaking and gently rubbing the air fryer with a cleaning sponge will help to remove all the browned bits and pieces of food that might stuck on the cooking surface.

6. **It is A Multi-Cooker:**

The air fryer does not only fries but also roasts, bakes, and grills. You can use the air fryer for breakfast, lunch and dinner.

7. **Safe to Use:**

Air fryer come with safety features. The manufactures built some safety features like auto shut down feature that can easily be used to shut down the machine when cooking. The closed cooking system also helps to avoid getting scalded by hot oil. The food is cooked inside the enclosed air fryer cooker.

8. **Fast and Convenient:**

The air fryer must not be preheated before cooking. Certain foods like frozen nuggets, French fries, potato wedges can be transferred from the freezer straight to the air fryer. Select the cooking temperature and timer and cook.

9. **Low Fat:**

There's no need of adding any oil when air frying frozen food for baking. No oil is required for raw meat too. You just have to take it from the freezer and add them straight into the air fryer basket, then adjust the temperature and timer.

Cleaning & Maintenance

Cleaning Your Air Fryer Max XL

- The air fryer should be thoroughly cleaned after each use.
- Unplug the unit from the wall outlet before cleaning.

NOTE: NEVER immerse the main unit in water or any other liquid. NEVER clean the main unit in a dishwasher.

- To clean the main unit and the control panel, wipe them clean with a paper towel or damp cloth.
- The basket, crisper plate, and any accessories can be washed in the dishwasher.
- If food residue is stuck on the crisper plate or basket, place them in a sink filled with warm, soapy water and soak for a couple of minutes.
- Pat dry with a paper towel or air-dry all parts after use.

1. **Don't Overcrowd the Basket:**

If you want your fried foods to turn out crispy, you'll have to avoid overcrowding the air fryer basket. Overloading/overcrowding the air fryer basket will prevent the hot distributed air from cooking the food. Placing too much food in the basket will prevent your food from crisping and browning.

To ensure this doesn't happen, cook your food in batches or invest in a bigger air fryer. Ensure that you turn or flip certain foods midway through the cooking process to crisp the entire surface of the food.

2. **Invest in a Good Quick Read Thermometer:**

It's vital to have a good quality quick read thermometer because it is very important in checking the temperature of certain foods like steak, chicken, and pork. Make use of a thermometer to get accurate reading of the temperature of certain foods like meat and chicken.

3. **Preheat your Air Fryer:**

The unit should be preheated before adding the ingredients. Some models of air fryers recommend that the cooking element should be preheated to ensure even cooking. If your air fryer does not have a preheat setting, simply turn it to the desired temperature and allow it to run for around 3 minutes before adding your food.

4. **Spray Midway Through Cooking:**

Spraying your food with oil midway through cooking gets the best crisp on most foods. I always spray my foods with little oil halfway through cooking unless it's an item that doesn't need spraying, like fatty meats. Coated food items and dry flour should be sprayed halfway through air frying.

5. **Shake the Basket during Cooking for fries, wings, etc.**

Shake the air fryer basket every few minutes when cooking smaller food items like chicken wings, French fries, to ensure even cooking. You can also use a pair of silicone kitchen tongs to turn or flip larger items in the basket.

6. **Grease your Air Fryer Basket:**

Even if your food does not require oil, always sprinkle some oil to grease the air fryer basket. You can brush, rub or spray with little bit of oil on the bottom grates to prevent your food from stuck to the bottom of the basket.

7. **Use Oil on Some Foods:**

Spraying some foods with oil will help them crisp but certain foods don't necessarily oil. Some foods like dark meat chicken, ground beef, fatty cuts of meat, etc. do not need oil. I also use oil on vegetables Air Fried Potatoes and seafoods.

CHAPTER ONE
BREAKFAST & BRUNCH RECIPES
Breakfast Sausage Wraps

Preparation time: 5 minutes

Cook time: 3 minutes

Total time: 8 minutes

Servings: 8

Ingredients:

- 8 sausages
- 2 pieces of American cheese
- 1 can Crescent Roll Dough, refrigerated Ketchup syrup for dipping

Cooking Instructions:

1. Separate Crescent Rolls in a flat working table and cut the cheese with a knife.
2. Add 1 Crescent Roll on the working table and begin working from the base of the triangle to the tip.
3. Add the cheese and sausage on the broad side of the triangle. Pull the triangle from the ends over the cheese and sausage.
4. Roll and tuck the remaining portion. Firmly pinch the dough to stay firm over the sausage and cheese.
5. Similarly, roll all the Crescent Rolls. Transfer the sausage wraps in the air fryer basket.
6. Set the air fryer to 380°F and start cooking for 3 minutes.
7. Serve with ketchup and enjoy!

Nutritional Information:

Calories: 169, Total fat: 11g, Saturated fat: 2.6g, Cholesterol:5mg, Sodium: 624mg, Total carbs: 9g, Dietary fiber: 2g, Sugars: 1g, Protein: 11g

Cranberry Pecan Muffins

Preparation time: 10 minutes

Cooking time: 15 minutes

Total time: 25 minutes

Servings: 8

Ingredients:

- ½ cup cranberries, fresh
- ¼ cup, diced pecans
- ¼ cup of dairy milk
- 2 eggs
- 1½ cup almond flour
- ½ tsp. vanilla extract
- 1 tsp. baking powder
- ¼ tsp. ground cinnamon
- ⅛ tsp. salt

Cooking Instructions:

1. Add together the eggs, vanilla, and milk in a blender jar. Blend for about 30 seconds. Add almond flour, baking powder, sugar, salt, and cinnamon.
2. Continue blending the ingredients for additional 45 seconds. Add the chopped pecans and cranberries and combine. Do not blend it using the blender.
3. Place the entire mix into muffin cups. Top it with fresh cranberries.
4. Add the muffins in the air fryer basket. Set the Air Fryer to 325°F and set the timer to 15 minutes.
5. Check the muffin for doneness by inserting a toothpick to come out clean.
6. Once cooked it has cooked through, remove it from the air fryer and allow to cool. Top with drizzling maple glaze before serving and enjoy!

Nutritional Information:

Calories: 72, Total fat: 5.2g, Saturated fat: 1.1g, Cholesterol: 155mg, Sodium: 68mg, Total carbs: 4g, Dietary fiber: 1g, Sugars: 3g, Protein: 3g

Breakfast Frittata

Preparation time: 15 minutes

Cook time: 20minutes

Total time 35 minutes

Servings: 2

Ingredients:

- 4 eggs
- 1 green onion, shredded
- ¼ pound sausage, cooked
- ½ cup Cheddar cheese, shredded
- 2 tbsp. red bell pepper, chopped
- ⅛ tsp. cayenne pepper Cooking spray

Cooking Instructions:

1. In a medium bowl, beat the eggs.
2. Crumble the sausages and set aside.
3. Add all the ingredients in a medium bowl and combine well.
4. Set your Ninja Air fryer to 360°F and preheat.
5. Spray the cake pan with cooking oil and put the mixture into it.
6. Set timer to 20 minutes.
7. Serve hot and enjoy!

Nutritional Information:

Calories: 380, Total Carbs: 2.9g, Dietary fiber: 0.4g, Total fat: 27.4g, Saturated fat: 12g, Cholesterol: 443mg, Sodium: 694mg, Potassium: 328mg, Protein: 31.2g, Sugars: 1g

Hash Brown

Preparation time: 15 minutes

Cook time: 30 minutes

Total time: 45 minutes

Servings: 4

Ingredients:

- 1½ pounds of potatoes, peeled and washed
- 1 red bell pepper, seeded.
- 1½ tablespoon olive oil
- 1 onion, small.
- 1 jalapeno, seeded.
- ½ tsp. taco seasoning mix
- ½ tsp. ground cumin
- ¼ tsp. ground black pepper
- ¼ tsp. salt

Cooking Instructions:

1. Cut the potatoes into 1-inch chunks and soak for 20 minutes. Cut bell pepper into 1-inch pieces. Cut onion into 1-inch cubes.
2. Chop jalapeno into one-inch rings. Drain the potatoes, dry it by using a towel and keep it ready in a medium bowl.
3. Sprinkle 1 tablespoon olive oil over it and toss the potatoes for proper coating. Set the Ninja Air Fryer to 320°F and preheat.
4. Put the potatoes in the air fry basket and cook for 18 minutes. Add together the chopped onion, pepper and jalapeno in a bowl.
5. Drizzle the remaining half tablespoon olive oil and toss. Add the cumin, taco seasoning, pepper and salt and toss to coat.
6. Take out the cooked potatoes from the air fryer basket and place it into the vegetable mixture bowl and toss.
7. Place the empty fryer basket into the air fryer. Increase the temperature to 356°F and preheat. Place the tossed vegetable and potato mixture back to the air fryer basket and cook for 6 minutes.
8. Shake the basket occasionally until the food becomes crispy.
9. Shake it and cook for another 5 minutes. Serve hot and enjoy!

Nutritional Information:

Calories: 186, Total Carbohydrate: 33.7g, Dietary fiber: 4.8g, Total fat: 4.3g, Saturated fat: 1g, Cholesterol: 0mg, Sodium: 79mg, Potassium: 817mg, Protein: 4g, Sugars: 3g, Calcium: 29mg

Quick French Toast Sticks

Preparation time: 10 minutes

Cook time: 10 minutes

Total time: 20 minutes

Servings: 2

Ingredients:

- 4 slices thick bread
- 2 eggs, beaten
- 1 tsp. vanilla extract
- ¼ cup milk
- ⅛ tsp. ground nutmeg
- 1 tsp. cinnamon
- Parchment paper

Cooking Instructions:

1. Place parchment paper into the bottom of the air fryer basket.
2. Cut the sliced bread into a stick shape.
3. Set the Ninja air fryer to 360°F.
4. Add together the vanilla, milk, egg, nutmeg, and cinnamon in a medium bowl. Give everything a good mix to combine.
5. Dredge the breadstick into the mix. Transfer them into the air fryer basket.
6. Do not overlap the sticks. Place it in a single layer.
7. Set the cooking timer to 5 minutes.
8. After 5 minutes, flip the side and cook additional 5 minutes.
9. Serve hot and enjoy!

Nutritional Information:

Calories: 231, Total carbs: 28.6g, Dietary fiber: 1.9g, Total fat: 7.4g, Saturated fat: 1g, Cholesterol: 188mg, Sodium: 423mg, Potassium: 173mg, Sugars: 4g, Protein: 11.2g, Calcium: 150mg

Sausage Patties

Preparation time: 5 minutes

Cook time: 10 minutes

Total time: 15 minutes

Servings: 4

Ingredients:

- 12 ounces sausage patties
- Non-stick cooking spray

Cooking Instructions:

1. Set the Ninja Air Fryer to 400°F and start preheating.
2. Add the sausage patties into the air fryer basket.
3. Place the sausage patties in a single layer and avoid overcrowding.
4. Set the timer to 5 minutes. Flip the patties after 5 minutes for additional 5 minutes.
5. Serve hot and enjoy!

Nutritional Information:

Calories: 145, Total carbs: 0.7g, Dietary fiber: 0g, Total fat: 9g, Saturated fat: 3g, Cholesterol: 46mg, Sodium: 393mg, Potassium: 228mg, Protein: 14.1g, Sugars: 1g, Calcium: 16mg.

Baked Apple

Preparation time: 5 minutes

Cook time: 20minutes

Total time: 25 minutes

Servings: 1

Ingredients:

- 1 apple, medium size
- 1½ tsp. melted, light margarine
- 2 tbsp. diced walnuts
- 2 tbsp. raisins
- ¼ tsp. nutmeg
- ¼ tsp. cinnamon
- ¼ cup of water

Cooking Instructions:

1. Set the Ninja Air Fryer to 350°F and start preheating.
2. Cut the apple from above the middle portion. Peel some apple flesh and make some room for the filling.
3. Place the apple at the bottom of the air fryer. In a medium bowl, combine all the ingredients.
4. Fill the mixture into the space provided in the apple.
5. Add quarter cup of water into the pan and bake for 20 minutes.
6. Serve hot and enjoy!

Nutritional Information:

Calories: 322, Total fat: 15.6, Saturated at: 1.6g, Cholesterol: 0mg, Sodium: 73mg, Total carbs: 40.5g, Dietary fiber: 7.6g, Sugars: 34.3g, Protein: 5g, Calcium: 30mg, Potassium: 464mg

Sweet Potato Hash

Preparation time: 10 minutes

Cook time: 15 minutes

Total time: 25 minutes

Serves: 6

Ingredients:

- 2 sweet potato, large, cut into chunks
- 2 tbsp. olive oil
- 2 slices bacon, sliced into tiny pieces
- 1 tbsp. smoked paprika
- 1 tsp. dried dill
- 1 tsp. ground black pepper
- 1 tsp. of sea salt

Cooking Instructions:

1. Set the Ninja Air Fryer oven to 400°F and preheat for the cooking.
2. In a medium bowl, add together all the ingredients and toss.
3. Open the air fryer and place the mixed ingredients in the ceramic-coated tray.
4. Set the timer for 12-16 minutes.
5. Open the tray after 10 minutes and stir the ingredients.
6. Repeat checking the food after every 4 minutes until the food are cooked through.
7. Once it is browned, select the stop button/stop mark.
8. Serve hot and enjoy!

Nutritional Information:

Calories 191, Carbohydrates: 34g, fat 6g, Protein: 3.7g, Cholesterol 3mg, Sodium: 447mg, Potassium: 566mg, Sugars: 6g, Saturated fat: 1.0g, Calcium: 52mg

Cinnamon Rolls

Preparation time: 20 minutes

Cooking time: 9minutes

Total time: 29 minutes

Servings: 8

Ingredients:

- ¾ cup brown sugar
- 1-pound bread dough, frozen, thawed
- ¼ cup butter, melted
- 1½ tablespoon ground cinnamon

Cream Cheese Glaze:

- 4 ounces cream cheese, melted in room temperature
- 1¼ cup sugar, powdered
- 2 tablespoons butter, softened in room temperature
- ½ teaspoon vanilla

Cooking Instructions:

1. Set the bread dough at room temperature to get thawed. Roll the dough on a floured working table to make a rectangle of 13x11 inches size.
2. Brush the melted butter on the surface of the dough, just one inch behind the edges. Avoid brushing the tips with butter.
3. In a medium bowl, combine together the cinnamon powder and brown sugar. Sprinkle the mix on the buttered surface of the dough.
4. Roll the dough without any air pockets. While reaching to the non-buttered area, press the dough to the roll to get it sealed.
5. Use a knife in cutting the roll into 8 pieces without flattening the dough. Cover it with a baking towel and set aside for 2 hours.
6. Add the butter and cheese in a microwave-safe bowl to make the glaze. Microwave it for 30 seconds.
7. Once it has become smooth, add the grounded sugar and give everything a good mix. Add vanilla and stir to combine.
8. Set aside. By the time the sliced rolls start to rise. Set the Ninja Air Fryer to 350°F and preheat. Transfer the rolls into the air basket.

9. Set the timer for 5 minutes and cook. Flip the rolls and cook for additional 4 minutes. After cooking, pour the cheese glaze on the rolls.

10. Serve hot and enjoy!

Nutritional Information:

Calories: 417, Total fat: 14.6g, Saturated fat: 8.4g, Trans fat: 0.4g, Cholesterol: 36mg, Sodium: 409mg, Total carbs: 67g, Dietary fiber: 2g, Sugars: 40g, Protein: 6g

Cinnamon and Sugar Doughnuts

Preparation time: 24minutes

Cooking time: 16 minutes

Total time: 40 minutes

Servings: 9

Ingredients:

- ½ + ⅓ cup white sugar
- 2 large egg yolks
- 1½ tsp. baking powder
- 2½ + 2 tbsp. butter, melted at room temperature
- 2¼ cup all-purpose flour
- ½ cup sour cream
- 1 tsp. cinnamon
- 1 tbsp. salt

Cooking Instructions:

1. Add together the 2½ tbsp. of butter and half cup white sugar in a medium bowl. Combine the ingredients until it becomes crumbly.
2. Add egg yolks and give everything a good stir to combine. In another bowl combine baking powder, all-purpose flour, and salt.
3. From the above mix, take ⅓ of the flour mix and add to the sugar-egg yolk mix.
4. Add half of the portion of sour cream also into the egg-sugar mix and combine the entire mix thoroughly.
5. Add all the remaining sour cream and flour mix. Combine thoroughly to become a dough. Refrigerate the dough for some time.
6. Mix the remaining ⅓ cup white sugar and cinnamon powder in another bowl.
7. Spread some flour on the working table and roll the dough over into making a half-inch-thick dough. The dough will be enough to make 9 circles.
8. Make a cutting at the center of the circle to look like a doughnut shape. Set the Ninja Air Fryer oven at 350°F and start preheating.
9. Brush the remaining melted butter on both sides of the doughnuts. Place the doughnuts in the frying basket without overlapping.
10. Bake for 8 minutes. Brush the cooked doughnuts with melted butter. Dip in the cinnamon and sugar mix. Bake the doughnuts in batches.

11. Serve and enjoy!

Calories: 276, Total Carbohydrates: 43.5g, Dietary Fiber: 1g, Cholesterol: 66mg, Total Fat: 9.7g, Saturated Fat: 6g, Sodium: 390mg, Potassium: 59mg, Protein: 4.3g, Sugars: 19g

Rotisserie Chicken

Preparation time: 10 minutes

Cooking time: 60 minutes

Total time: 1 hour 10 minutes

Servings: 2

Ingredients:

- 1 (4 pounds) whole chicken
- ½ tsp. salt
- ½ tsp. ground black pepper
- 2 tbsp. classified butter
- 1 tbsp. magic mushroom powder
- Cooking spray

Cooking Instructions:

1. Remove the giblets and pat dry with a paper towel. In a medium bowl, mix ghee and mushroom powder.

2. Pull back the skin from the chicken's breast area and fill in the ghee mixture using a spoon. Coat it evenly in the insides of the chicken too.

3. Once coated well, season the chicken with salt and pepper. Spray cooking oil over the chicken.

4. Add the chicken in the air fryer basket. Set the air fryer basket at 365° F and cook for 30 minutes.

5. After 30 minutes, turn the chicken, and spritz some cooking spray. Cook the chicken for additional 30 minutes.

6. Serve the chicken in slices and enjoy!

Nutritional Information:

Calories: 1115, Total carbs: 1g, Dietary fiber: 0g, Sugars: 1g, Protein: 185g, Total fat: 36.1g, Saturated fat: 13.4g, Trans fat: 0.5g, Cholesterol: 620mg, Sodium: 1397mg

Mediterranean Breaded Chicken

Preparation time: 5 minutes

Cooking time: 20 minutes

Total time: 25 minutes

Servings: 2

Ingredients:

- 2 chicken breasts, skinless
- 1 egg, small
- 1 tsp. thyme
- 1 tsp. salt
- 3 ounces Tuscan herb granola
- 1 tsp. ground pepper

Cooking Instructions:

1. Wash and pat dry the chicken breasts. Chop the chickens into bite sizes like chicken nuggets.
2. In a small bowl, beat the egg. Transfer the Tuscan granola in a sandwich bag and bash it with a rolling pin to create a mix of fine and medium chunks.
3. Add the salt, pepper, and thyme in the sandwich bag with the granola.
4. Transfer the granola mixture into a shallow bowl. Coat the chicken chunks in the beaten egg and then dredge it in the granola mixture.
5. Press down the mixture on the chicken chunks to have a better coating on the chicken chunks. Place the chicken pieces in the air fryer basket without overlapping.
6. Sprinkle the chicken pieces with some cooking oil. Cook the chicken at 360° F for 10 minutes. After 10 minutes of cooking, flips the chicken pieces and spray some cooking oil.
7. Continue frying for additional 10 minutes.
8. Serve warm with the desired sauce and enjoy!

Nutritional Information:

Calories: 764, Total fat: 42g, Saturated fat: 15.6g, Trans fat: 0.3g, Cholesterol: 261mg, Sodium: 1456mg, Total carbs: 25g, Dietary fiber: 2g, Sugars: 11g, Protein: 67g

Chicken Breast

Preparation time: 2 minutes

Cooking time: 20 minutes

Total time: 22 minutes

Servings: 4

Ingredients:

- 4 chicken breast, boneless, skinless
- ½ tsp. black pepper
- ½ tsp. oregano, dried
- ½ tsp. garlic powder
- ½ tsp. salt
- Cooking spray

Cooking Instructions:

1. Wash the chicken breasts and pat dry.
2. Combine together the salt, garlic powder, pepper, and oregano in a medium bowl. Add the chicken breasts in a shallow bowl and spray some cooking oil.
3. Sprinkle the prepared seasoning mixture over the chicken breasts and rub it. Arrange the chicken on the air fryer basket as it is upside down.
4. Spray the other side of the chicken with cooking oil and apply the seasoning mixture over it. Set the air fryer at 360° F.
5. Cook the chicken breast for 10 minutes. Depending upon the size of the chicken, flip the pieces to cook the other side, and continue cooking for 10 minutes.
6. Remove the basket from the air fryer and allow the chicken cool down.
7. Cut the cooked chicken into your desired sizes.
8. Serve warm with your desired sauce.

Nutritional Information:

Calories: 163, Fat: 3g, Protein: 30g, Cholesterol: 90mg, Sodium:454mg, Potassium: 522mg, Calcium: 11mg

Seasoned Chicken Breast

Preparation time: 10 minutes

Cooking time: 15 minutes

Total time: 25 minutes

Servings: 1

Ingredients:

- 4 chicken breasts, skinless
- 2 tbsp. of olive oil
- 2 tbsp. Creole, to season

Cooking Instructions:

1. Wash chicken and pat dry with a paper towel. Place a piece of an aluminum foil in the inner bottom of the air fryer.

2. Trim the sizes of the chicken into bite sizes. Brush the chicken pieces with olive oil on both the sides

3. Sprinkle the seasoning on every chicken piece and pat down the seasoning thoroughly. Add the breast in the air fryer basket, without overlapping.

4. Set the air fryer temperature at 390° F to cook for 8 minutes. After 8 minutes of cooking, turn the chicken to cook on other side.

5. Sprinkle some cooking oil over the chicken and cook for 8 minutes. Check the chicken for tenderness before removing for serving.

6. Serve and enjoy!

Nutritional Information:

Calories 261, Carbohydrates: 1g, Fat 11g, Protein: 37g, Cholesterol 102mg, Sodium: 2368mg, Sugars: 0g, Saturated fat: 2g.

Chicken Wings

Preparation time: 10 minutes

Cooking time: 40 minutes

Total time: 50 minutes

Servings: 2

Ingredients:

- 2 pounds of chicken wings
- 4 tablespoons butter, melted
- 2 teaspoons blue cheese dressing, to serve
- 6-ounce franks, red hot sauce
- Cooking spray,
- canola oil

Cooking Instructions:

1. Separate flats from the drumettes and remove the tips of chicken wings. Wash, pat dry, and set aside.
2. Sprinkle the air fryer basket with cooking spray and on the chicken wings. Add the chicken wings in the basket.
3. Set the air fryer temperature at 400° F and preheat for 10 minutes. Add the chicken wings in the air fryer basket without overlapping.
4. Cook for 10 minutes. Flip the chicken wings midway through the cooking. Once done, spritz some more cooking oil and cook for 6 minutes.
5. In a medium bowl, add the melted butter with the hot sauce and mix it thoroughly. Then, toss the chicken wings in the spicy red sauce.
6. Dress blue cheese on top and serve.

Nutritional Information:

Calories: 842, Cholesterol: 321mg, Total fat: 41.7g, Saturated fat: 19.3g, Trans fat: 1.3g, Sodium: 1274mg, Total carbs: 11g, Dietary fiber: 0g, Sugars: 6g, Protein: 100g

Crispy Italian Chicken

Preparation time: 20 minutes

Cooking time: 50 minutes

Total time: 1 hour 10 minutes

Servings: 4

Ingredients:

- 1¼-pound chicken thighs
- 2 tsp. basil leaves, fresh, thinly sliced
- 2 tbsp. olive oil, extra virgin
- ⅛ tsp. ground black pepper
- 8 tsp. baby arugulas
- 5 cherry tomatoes, halved
- 2 tsp. all-purpose flour
- 2 tbsp. balsamic vinegar
- 1 egg, large
- ½ tsp. salt
- 15-20 tsp. breadcrumbs
- 6 tsp. parmesan cheese, grated
- Cooking spray

Cooking Instructions:

1. Wash the chicken and pat dry. Cut a parchment paper in round shape and place it in the air fryer basket.
2. Let us make 3 marinade stations using a shallow dish.
3. Add the flour in the first shallow dish. Beat together the egg, vinegar, and the ¼ salt in another shallow bowl.
4. In the third shallow dish, mix the bread crumbs and the parmesan cheese.
5. Then, coat the chicken one by one, dip it in the flour and shake off excess flour.
6. Then, dip in the egg mixture and lastly dredge in the bread crumbs mixture.
7. Repeat the procedure for all the chicken thighs and press the crumbs well over the chicken. Spray some cooking oil on the coated chicken.
8. Add the chicken in the parchment paper, which is already in the air fryer basket. Set the temperature to 325°F and cook for 15 minutes.

9. Flip the chicken midway through the cooking and spritz some cooking oil. Cook for additional 10 minutes.

10. Drizzle some basil on top of the chicken. In a large bowl, mix the olive oil, vinegar, ¼ teaspoon salt, and the pepper.

11. Pour over the tomatoes and arugulas, toss and coat them thoroughly.

12. Serve as a salad with the chicken.

Nutritional Information:

Calories 390, Carbohydrates: 22g, Fat 17g, Protein: 36g, Cholesterol 190mg, Sodium:860mg, Potassium: 460mg, Sugars: 3g, Saturated fat: 4.5g, Calcium: 9g

Whole Chicken

Preparation time: 5 minutes

Cooking time: 60 minutes

Total time: 1 hour 5 minutes

Servings: 6

Ingredients:

- 1 (4 pounds) whole chicken, giblets removed
- 1 tsp. paprika, smoked
- ½ tsp. oregano, dried
- ½ tsp. basil, dried
- 2 tbsp. avocado oil
- 1 tsp. ground black pepper
- 1 tsp. kosher salt
- ½ tsp. thyme, dried
- Cooking spray

Cooking Instructions:

1. Wash chicken and pat dry with a paper towel.
2. In a medium bowl, combine together all the seasoning and add some oil. Spread it evenly over the chicken.
3. Pat it down and ensure that the chicken is evenly coated. Spray the air fryer basket with some cooking oil. Add the chicken in the basket.
4. Cook for about 50 minutes at 360° F until the chicken gets tender. Flip the chicken midway through the cooking.
5. Serve hot with sauce and enjoy!

Nutritional Information:

Calories: 380, Total fat: 12.9g, Saturated fat: 2.6g, Trans fat: 0g, Cholesterol: 197mg, Sodium: 615mg, Total carbs: 1g, Dietary fiber: 0g, Sugars: 0g, Protein: 62g

Baked Tuscan Chicken

Preparation time: 1 hours

Cooking time: 35 minutes

Total time: 1 hour 35 minutes

Servings: 4

Ingredients:

- 4 chicken breasts, boneless, skinless
- 1 tbsp. oregano, dried, minced
- ½ onion, yellow, minced
- 3 garlic cloves, minced
- 3 sun-dried tomatoes, diced
- 1 tsp. salt
- 1 tsp. pepper
- 4 tsp. extra virgin olive oil
- 6 tbsp. lemon juice
- 1 tbsp. rosemary, freshly minced
- 1 tbsp. thyme, freshly minced
- 1 lemon, thinly sliced
- Cooking spray

Cooking Instructions:

1. Wash chicken and pat dry with a paper towel. In a saucepan, add the olive oil, herbs, lemon juice, onion, and bring to boil in low heat.

2. Continue stirring until the onions become transparent. Add the garlic and the sun-dried tomatoes in the saucepan along with salt and pepper.

3. Stir and continue cooking for at least 2-3 minutes. Once done, remove the saucepan and allow to cool for a couple of minutes.

4. Add the chicken breast in a baking dish and add this mixture over the chicken. Cover the dish and refrigerate it overnight.

5. Preheat the oven at 375° F for 5 minutes. Add the marinated chicken in the air fryer baking tray along with the marinades.

6. Place the lemon pieces over the chicken breast. Sprinkle with extra salt on top of the chicken and bake it for 30-35 minutes at 375°F.

7. After cooking, allow the chicken cool for a couple of minutes and slice it as desired. Serve and enjoy!

Nutritional Information:

Calories: 565, Carbs: 11g, Dietary fiber: 2g, Sugars: 2g, Total fat: 29.4g, Saturated fat: 8.1g, Trans fat: 0.3g, Cholesterol: 187mg, Sodium: 824mg

Blackened Chicken Breast

Preparation time: 10 minutes

Cooking time: 20 minutes

Total time: 30 minutes

Servings: 2

Ingredients:

- 2 (12 ounces) chicken breast, skinless and boneless
- ½ tsp. onion powder
- ½ tsp. ground black pepper
- ¼ tsp. salt
- 2 tsp. paprika
- 1 tsp. ground thyme1 teaspoon ground cumin
- ½ tsp. cayenne pepper powder
- 2 tsp. vegetable oil
- Cooking spray.

Cooking Instructions:

1. Wash and pat the chicken with a paper towel.
2. In a medium bowl, mix thyme, cayenne pepper, paprika, black pepper, cumin, and salt. Sprinkle oil over the chicken breasts.
3. Then, dredge the chicken breast in the spice mixture kept in the medium bowl. Press and hold the spices into the chicken pieces for an evenly coating.
4. Allow it to get marinated for a couple of minutes. Set the air fryer temperature to 360°F and preheat for 5 minutes.
5. Add the coated chicken breast in the air fryer basket and cook for 10 minutes.
6. After 10 minutes of cooking, turn the chicken and spray with some cooking oil.
7. Continue cooking for additional 10 minutes.
8. Serve warm and enjoy!

Nutritional Information:

Calories: 432, Total fat: 9.5g, Saturated fat: 2g, Cholesterol: 198mg, Sodium: 516mg, Potassium: 968mg, Total carbs: 3.2g, Dietary fiber: 1.5g, Protein: 79.4g, Sugars: 1g, Calcium: 70mg

Panko Chicken

Preparation time: 5 minutes

Cooking time: 45 minutes

Total time: 50 minutes

Servings: 6

Ingredients:

- 6 chicken breast, skinless, boneless
- 1 tsp. salt
- ¾ tsp. ground black pepper
- pepper
- ½ tsp. cayenne5 tsp. butter, unsalted, melted
- 15 tbsp. panko bread crumbs
- Cooking spray

Cooking Instructions:

1. Wash chicken and pat dry with paper towel.
2. In a pie plate, mix breadcrumbs, cayenne pepper, salt, and black pepper.
3. Combine together the melted butter with salt and black pepper in a medium bowl. Brush this mixture over the chicken.
4. Once done, dredge the chicken in the crumbs mixture one by one and coat it thoroughly. Sprinkle the air fryer basket with some cooking oil.
5. Add the chicken breast in the basket without overlapping. Spray some cooking oil over the chicken.
6. Set the air fryer at 360°F and cook for 15 minutes. Turn the chicken midway through the cooking and spritz some cooking oil.
7. Serve warm with your desired sauce.

Nutritional Information:

Calories: 829, Total fat: 33.8g, Saturated fat: 10.5g, Trans fat: 0.5g, Cholesterol: 194mg, Sodium: 1147mg, Total carbs: 56g, Dietary fiber: 3g, Sugars: 7g, Protein: 71g

CHAPTER THREE
BEEF & PORK RECIPES
Perfect Steak

Preparation time: 20 minutes

Cooking time: 12 minutes

Total time: 32 minutes

Servings: 4

Ingredients:

- 2 (16 ounces) rib eye steak
- 1 tsp. salt
- 1 stick butter, unsalted
- 2 tbsp. parsley, fresh
- 2 tsp. garlic, minced
- 1 tsp. Worcestershire sauce
- ½ tsp. black pepper, freshly cracked
- 2 tbsp. olive oil
- ½ tsp. salt

Cooking Instructions:

1. In a medium bowl, combine together the butter, parsley, garlic, salt and Worcestershire sauce to make the garlic butter.
2. Defrost the steak and add olive oil on both the sides. Season the steak with salt and pepper. Set the air fryer at 400°F and preheat for 5 minutes.
3. Spray the air fryer basket with some olive oil. Add the steaks in the air fryer and spritz cooking oil. Cook the steak for 12 minutes.
4. Halfway through the cooking, turn it and spray some cooking oil. Transfer it to a bowl when done and allow to cool for a couple of minutes.
5. Serve hot with garlic butter over the steak.

Nutritional Information:

Calories 372, Total fat: 31.9g, Saturated fat: 12.3g, Trans fat: 1.5g, Cholesterol: 82mg, Sodium: 963mg, Total carbs: 1g, Dietary fiber: 0g, Sugars: 0g, Protein: 21g

Greek Lamb Chops

Preparation time: 5 minutes

Cooking time: 30 minutes

Total time: 35 minutes

Servings: 4

Ingredients:

- 6 Lamb chops, shoulder
- 1 potato, medium
- 1 lemon, medium
- 10 garlic cloves
- 1 tbsp oregano
- 1 lemon, large
- ½ tsp. salt
- ½ tsp. pepper
- 1 tbsp. olive oil

Cooking Instructions:

1. Clean, peel and cut the potatoes in cubes. Add the garlic cloves in a Zip lock bag along with olive oil, 1 medium lemon juiced and oregano.
2. Add the lamb chops and potatoes in the Zip lock bag and shake to coat the potatoes and meat with the marinade.
3. Transfer the bag in the refrigerator for at least 2 hours or allow to marinate overnight. Take the lamb chops out and remove the marinade.
4. Place the lamb chops in the air fryer pan and add the leftover garlic of the marinade over the meat.
5. Season with pepper and salt to taste. Add the lemon slices at the corners.
6. Add the potatoes along with some garlic cloves in the air fryer pan. Set the air fryer timer to 25 minutes at 360°F.
7. Turn the chops midway through the cooking and continue cooking.
8. Serve hot and enjoy!

Nutritional Information:

Calories 652, Carbohydrates: 22g, Fat 49g, Protein: 32g, Cholesterol 125mg, Sodium: 110mg, Potassium: 962mg, Sugars: 1g, Saturated fat: 20g, Calcium: 103mg

Garlic Rosemary Lamb Chops

Preparation time: 3 minutes

Cooking time: 12 minutes

Total time: 15 minutes

Servings: 4

Ingredients:

- 4 lamb chops
- 2 teaspoons garlic puree
- 2 teaspoons olive oil
- 1 teaspoon rosemary, fresh
- 3 garlic cloves, fresh
- ½ teaspoon salt
- 1 teaspoon pepper
- Cooking spray.

Cooking Instructions:

1. Brush the lamb chops with olive oil. Season the meat with salt and pepper.
2. Add the garlic puree on each lamb chop. Refrigerate the marinated lamb chops for at least 1 hour.
3. Half an hour before cooking, remove them from the fridge. Transfer the chops on the air fryer grill pan. Sprinkle rosemary and garlic cloves over the chops.
4. Place the grill pan in the air fryer and set the air fryer at 360°F. Cook for 6 minutes.
5. Flip the chops around after 6 minutes and allow to cook for more 6 minutes.
6. Repeat for any frozen meat. Discard the rosemary and garlic from the dish.
7. Allow it to cool for a couple of minutes before serving.
8. Serve warm and enjoy!

Nutritional Information:

Calories 208, Carbohydrates: 2g, Total fat 10.9g, Protein: 25g, Cholesterol 83mg, Sodium: 389mg, Sugars: 1g, Saturated fat: 3.8g, Dietary fiber: 0g

Meatloaf

Preparation time: 10 minutes

Cooking time: 25 minutes

Total time: 45 minutes

Servings: 4

Ingredients:

- 1-pound ground beef, lean
- 1 tbsp. thyme, freshly chopped
- 1 tsp. salt
- ½ tsp. black pepper, ground
- 2 mushrooms, thickly sliced
- 3 tbsp. bread crumbs
- 1 egg, medium, lightly beaten
- 1 onion, small, finely chopped
- 1 tbsp. olive oil

Cooking Instructions:

1. Set the air fryer at 390°F and preheat for 5 minutes.
2. Combine together the ground beef with egg, bread crumbs, thyme, onion, salt, and pepper in a medium bowl.
3. Transfer the beef mixture in the baking pan and smoothen the top layer.
4. Press the mushrooms at the top and brush with olive oil.
5. Place the pan in the air fryer basket. Set the cooking time to 25 minutes and roast the meatloaf inside until it becomes brown.
6. Once done, allow it to cool for a couple of minutes before slicing them into wedges. Serve and enjoy!

Nutritional Information:

Calories 297, Carbohydrates: 5.9g, Fat 18.8g, Protein: 24.8g, Cholesterol 126mg, Sodium: 706mg, Potassium: 361mg, Sugars: 1g, Saturated fat: 6.0g, Calcium: 33mg

Mongolian Beef

Preparation time: 20 minutes

Cooking time: 20 minutes

Total time: 40 minutes

Servings: 4

Ingredients:

- 1-pound steak, flank
- ¼ cup corn starch
- ½ cup green beans, chopped
- ½ cup green onions, chopped
- 2 teaspoons vegetable oil
- ½ teaspoon grated ginger
- ½ cup soy sauce
- ½ cup rice, cooked
- 1 tablespoon garlic, minced
- ½ cup water
- ¾ cup brown sugar

Cooking Instructions:

1. Rinse and pat dry the steak. Slice the steak in long pieces and coat it with corn starch. Add the meat in the air fryer.

2. Cook at 390°F for at least 5 minutes on each side. Sauté the sauce ingredients in a medium saucepan on medium-high heat.

3. Continue whisking the ingredients until the mixture comes to a boil. Once the steak is ready, add the steak in the bowl of sauce.

4. Allow the meat to soak the sauce for about 5-10 minutes. Remove the steak with tongs and allow the sauce drip off.

5. Place the meat over cooked rice and beans, top it with sauce if desired.

6. Serve and enjoy!

Nutritional Information:

Calories 554, Carbohydrates: 57g, Fat 16g, Protein: 44g, Cholesterol 116mg, Sodium: 2211mg, Sugars: 35g, Saturated fat: 5g

Beef Steak Kabobs

Preparation time: 30 minutes

Cooking time: 10 minutes

Total time: 40 minutes

Servings: 4

Ingredients:

- 1-pound beef
- 2 tablespoons soy sauce
- 1 bell pepper, chopped
- ½ Onion, chopped
- 2 tablespoons soy sauce
- 1 bell pepper, chopped
- ⅓ cup sour cream, low-fat
- 8 bamboo skewers

Cooking Instructions:

1. Rinse beef, discard ribs and cut into 1" pieces
2. Whisk together the sour cream with soy sauce in a medium bowl. Add the beef chunk and allow to marinate for at least 30 minutes.
3. Chop the onions and bell pepper in 1-inch pieces. Soak the skewers in water for at least 10 minutes.
4. Gently thread the bell pepper, onions and beef in the skewers and sprinkle black with pepper.
5. Set the air fryer temperature at 400°F and cook for 10 minutes. Turn the meat around halfway.
6. Serve and enjoy!

Nutritional Information:

Calories 250, Carbohydrates: 4g, Fat 15g, Protein: 23g, Cholesterol 84mg, Sodium: 609mg, Potassium: 519mg, Sugars: 2g, Saturated fat: 6.0g, Calcium: 49mg.

Steak with Portobello Mushrooms

Preparation time: 5 minutes

Cooking time: 10 minutes

Total time: 15 minutes

Servings: 2

Ingredients:

- 2 strip steaks, cut in ¾ inch pieces
- 2 tsp. Montreal steak seasoning
- 4 ounces Portobello mushrooms, chopped in quarters
- 3 tbsp. olive oil
- ½ tsp. garlic powder
- 1 tbsp. coconut amino

Cooking Instructions:

1. Combine together the coconut amino, olive oil, steak seasoning and garlic powder in a medium bowl.
2. Give the ingredients a good stir and add steak pieces in it. Allow to marinate for 15 minutes. Set the air fryer at 390°F for 5 minutes.
3. Layer a perforated parchment paper at the bottom of the air fryer. Drain the steak from the marinade and discard off any excess.
4. Put it along with the Portobello mushrooms in the air fryer basket.
5. Cook in the air fryer for 5 minutes. Remove the basket and toss the steak and mushrooms a little. Cook for additional 5 minutes.
6. Serve hot and enjoy!

Nutritional Information:

Calories 548, Carbohydrates: 4.9g, Fat 40.1g, Protein: 41g, Cholesterol 98mg, Sodium: 731mg, Potassium: 777mg, Sugars: 1g, Saturated fat: 9.0g, Calcium: 35mg

Steak with Roasted Potatoes

Preparation time: 5 minutes

Cooking time: 36 minutes

Total time: 41 minutes

Servings: 1

Ingredients:

- ½ pound strip loin steak
- 4 potatoes, small, chopped
- ½ tsp. salt
- 1 tsp. pepper
- 1 tbsp. of olive oil
- 1 tsp. cayenne pepper
- 1 tsp. salt
- 1 tsp. Italian herbs
- ½ tbsp. olive oil
- Cooking spray

Cooking Instructions:

1. Add together the cayenne pepper, olive oil, Italian herbs, salt and potatoes in a medium bowl. Set the air fryer temperature at 365°F preheat for 5 minutes.
2. Add the potatoes in the air fryer basket and spray some cooking oil. Cook the potatoes for 16 minutes.
3. Shake the basket midway through the cooking. Set the potatoes aside once it has done. Transfer the steak on a flat surface and rub salt and pepper with oil.
4. Rub over both the sides. Spray some cooking oil on the steak. Cook at 390°F for 12 minutes. After 12 minutes, turn the steak and spray some cooking oil.
5. Cooking the steak for additional 8 minutes.
6. Serve warm with the potatoes and enjoy!

Nutritional Information:

Calories: 433, Total fat: 20.8g, Saturated fat: 5.6g, Trans fat: 0.6g, Cholesterol: 96mg, Sodium: 1818mg, Total carbs: 24g, Dietary fiber: 3g, Sugars: 2g, Protein: 36g

Lamb Chops

Preparation time: 5 minutes

Cooking time: 25 minutes

Total time: 30 minutes

Servings: 2

Ingredients:

- 2 lamb chops, medium
- 2 teaspoons lemon juice Cooking spray

Cooking Instructions:

1. Set the air fryer at 350°F and preheat for 3 minutes.
2. Spritz cooking oil in the air fryer basket. Add the lamb chops in the air fryer basket and spray cooking oil.
3. Cook the meat for 25 minutes. Midway through the cooking, flip and spray some cooking oil.
4. Once done, allow it to cool for about 10 minutes. Drizzle lemon juice over the lamb before serving.
5. Serve and enjoy!

Nutritional Information:

Calories 330, Carbohydrates: 45g, fat 6g, Protein: 25g, Sodium: 1250mg, Sugars: 1g, Saturated fat: 2g

Lamb Loin Chops

Preparation time: 5 minutes

Cooking time: 25 minutes

Total time: 30 minutes

Servings: 2

Ingredients:

- 2 lamb chops, medium
- 3 teaspoon lemon juice, optional
- Cooking spray

Cooking Instructions:

1. Rinse and pat the lamb chops dry with a paper towel.
2. Set the air fryer temperature to 350°F and preheat for 3 minutes.
3. Spray the air fryer basket with some cooking oil. Place the lamb chops in the air fryer basket and spritz some cooking oil on it.
4. Cook the chops for at least 25 minutes. Half way through the cooking, turn the chops to coat evenly and spray some cooking oil.
5. After cooking, allow it to cool for a couple of minutes. Drizzle some lemon juice over the meat.
6. Serve with your desired side dish and enjoy!

Nutritional Information:

Calories: 163, Total fat: 7.8g, Saturated fat: 3.1g, Trans fat: 0.3g, Cholesterol: 75mg, Sodium: 87mg, Total carbs: 1g, Dietary fiber: 0g, Sugars: 0g, Protein: 23g

CHAPTER FOUR
FISH & SEAFOODS
Crispy Cod Nuggets

Preparation time: 10 minutes

Cooking time: 15 minutes

Total time: 25 minutes

Servings: 4

Ingredients:

- 1½ pounds cod fillets.
- ½ teaspoon ground pepper
- ¼ teaspoon salt
- 1 egg
- 1 tablespoon water
- 1 tablespoon vegetable oil
- Cooking spray
- ½ cup flour
- ½ cup cracker crumbs

Cooking Instructions:

1. Cut the cod fillets into 8 pieces. Crush the crackers in a food blender to fine crumbs. Add 1 tbsp. of vegetable oil and give everything a good mix.
2. Add the fine crumbs in a shallow bowl. Add the flour in a shallow bowl. Beat the egg and add 1 tbsp. of water in a medium bowl.
3. Rub pepper and salt on the fish fillet. Dredge the fish in the crumbs. Dip the fish fillet in the beaten egg mixture.
4. Then, dredge the fish fillet crumb powder. Set the air fryer temperature to 360°F. Spray some cooking oil in the air fryer basket.
5. Add the nuggets on the air fryer basket without overlapping and cook for 15 minutes. Halfway through the cooking toss the nuggets for better baking.
6. Serve hot along with sauce and salads.

Nutritional Information:

Calories: 325, Total fat: 26g, Saturated fat: 4g, Cholesterol: 58mg, Carbs: 21g, Sodium: 349mg, Dietary fiber: 1g, Sugars: 11g, Protein: 3g

Coconut Shrimp

Preparation time: 15 minutes

Cooking time: 15 minutes

Total time: 30 minutes

Servings: 4

Ingredients:

- 12 ounces (24 Shrimps), medium peeled, raw, with the tail on
- ½ cup all-purpose flour
- ⅓ cup breadcrumbs
- ½ tsp. kosher salt
- ¼ cup honey
- ¼ cup lime juice
- 1 Serrano Chile, thinly sliced
- 2 tsp. cilantro, freshly chopped Cooking spray
- 1 ½ tsp. black pepper, crushed
- 2 large Eggs
- ⅔ cup shredded coconut, unsweetened

Cooking Instructions:

1. Rinse the shrimps and pat dry with a paper towel. In a medium bowl, combine together the flour and pepper.
2. In a separate bowl, lightly beat 2 eggs. In a third shallow dish, mix the coconut flakes and breadcrumbs.
3. Then, take the shrimps one at a time, and dredge it in the flour mixture. After the flour mix, discard the excess and dip the shrimp in the beaten egg and dredge in the coconut mixture.
4. Press it down well so that the shredded coconut gets stick to the shrimp evenly.
5. Repeat the procedure for the remaining shrimps. Add the shrimps in the air fryer basket. Set the air fryer to 400°F and cook for 6-8 minutes or until golden.
6. Flip the shrimps when they're halfway cooked. Sprinkle some salt over the shrimps.
7. Meanwhile, whisk together the lime juice, honey, and Serrano Chile in a medium bowl to make the sauce.
8. Serve the shrimps hot with sprinkled cilantro and sauce.

Nutritional Information:

Calories 250, Carbohydrates: 30g, Fat 9g, Protein: 15g, Cholesterol 41mg, Sodium: 527mg, Potassium: 12mg, Sugars: 18g, Saturated fat: 7g, Calcium: 29mg

Crumbed Fish

Preparation time: 10 minutes

Cooking time: 12 minutes

Total time: 22 minutes

Serving: 4

Ingredients:

- 4 white fish fillets
- 1 lemon sliced
- 1 egg, beaten
- ¼ cup of vegetable oil
- 1 cup breadcrumbs

Cooking Instructions:

1. Set the air fryer to 350°F for 5 minutes.
2. In a medium bowl, add together the vegetable oil and bread crumbs and mix it until it forms a loose pattern.
3. Dip the fish fillets in the beaten egg, drop off any excess and dredge the fish fillets in the bread crumb mixture.
4. Ensure that the fillets are coated and evenly with the bread crumbs.
5. Place the fillets in the air fryer basket and cooking for at least 12 minutes.
6. Flip the fillets halfway through the cooking.
7. Garnish the fillets with lemon slides around it.
8. Serve hot and enjoy!

Nutritional Information:

Calories 354, Carbohydrates: 22.5g, fat 17.7g, Protein: 26.9g, Cholesterol 107mg, Sodium: 309mg, Potassium: 415mg, Sugars: 2g, Saturated fat: 3.0g, Calcium: 89mg.

Parmesan Shrimp

Preparation time: 10 minutes

Cooking time: 10 minutes

Total time: 20 minutes

Servings: 4

Ingredients:

- 2 lb. peeled, deveined and cooked shrimp
- ⅔ cup shredded parmesan cheese
- 1 tsp. ground pepper
- ½ tsp. oregano
- 1 tsp. onion powder
- 2 tbsp. olive oil
- 1 Lemon
- 4 cloves garlic, minced
- 1 tsp. basil
- Nonstick cooking spray

Cooking Instructions:

1. Quarter the lemon and set aside. Rinse the shrimp and pat dry with a paper towel.
2. In a medium bowl, mix together the grated cheese, garlic, oregano, pepper, olive oil, onion powder, and basil.
3. Add shrimp into the bowl and toss to coat the ingredients. Spray non-stick cooking oil in the air fryer basked.
4. Add the seasoned shrimps in the basket. Set the air fryer to 350°F. Cook for 10 minutes, until the seasoning on the shrimps gets brown.
5. Halfway through the cooking, shake the basket for even baking.
6. Squeeze lemon while serving.

Nutritional Information:

Calories; 179, Total fat: 7.4g, Saturated fat: 1.1g, Cholesterol: 0mg, Sodium: 5mg, Total carbs: 30.9g, Dietary fiber: 3.3g, Total sugars: 23.2g, Protein: 1g, Calcium: 28mg, Potassium: 233mg

Roasted Salmon with Fennel Salad

Preparation time: 10 minutes

Cooking time: 15 minutes

Total time: 25 minutes

Servings: 4

Ingredients:

- 6 ounces (4 Nos.) salmon fillets, skinless 2 teaspoon parsley, finely chopped.
- 1 tsp. thyme, freshly chopped
- 4 cups fennel, thinly sliced
- ⅔ cup Greek yogurt, low-fat
- 1 garlic clove, grated
- 2 tbsp. orange juice, freshly squeezed
- 1 tsp. lemon juice, freshly squeezed
- 1 tsp. divided kosher salt
- 2 tbsp. olive oil
- 2 tbsp. fresh dill, chopped

Cooking Instructions:

1. Set the air fryer to 360°F and preheat for 5 minutes.
2. In a medium bowl, combine together the parsley, thyme and ½ teaspoon salt.
3. Brush oil on the salmon fillets and sprinkle the marinade mixture.
4. Add the salmon fillets in an air fryer basket. Cook the salmon fillets at 360°F for at least 10 minutes.
5. Flip the fillets halfway through the cooking.
6. In a separate bowl, add together the remaining ingredients like fennel, garlic, yogurt, lemon juice, orange juice, dill and salt.
7. Give the ingredients a good stir for creating the fennel salad.
8. Serve salmon hot with the fennel salad.

Nutritional Information:

Calories 464, Carbohydrates: 9g, Fat 30g, Protein: 38g, Cholesterol 47mg, Sodium: 635mg, Potassium: 73mg, Sugars: 5g, Saturated fat: 7g, Calcium: 32mg.

Southern Style Catfish with Green Beans

Preparation time: 5 minutes

Cooking time: 20 minutes

Total time: 25 minutes

Servings: 2

Ingredients:

- 6-ounces catfish
- 12 ounces of green beans, small, freshly trimmed
- 1 tsp. brown sugar, light
- ⅓ cup breadcrumbs
- ¼ tsp. ground black pepper
- 2 tbsp. mayonnaise
- 1½ tsp. fresh dill, finely chopped
- ¾ tsp. of relish dill pickle
- ½ tsp. of apple cider vinegar
- ⅛ tsp. sugar, granulated
- ½ tsp. red pepper, freshly crushed
- ½ tsp. kosher salt, divided
- ¼ cup all-purpose flour
- 1 large egg, lightly beaten
- 1 lemon sliced to wedges
- 1 Cooking spray

Cooking Instructions:

1. Clean, rinse catfish. Pat dry with a paper towel. In a medium bowl, add the green beans and spray with some cooking oil.
2. Sprinkle some brown sugar, salt, crushed red pepper, and mix it well. Place the beans in the air fryer basket.
3. Set the air fryer temperature to 400°F and cook for at least 12 minutes or until it becomes tender.
4. Once done, transfer it in a separate bowl and cover with a piece of aluminum foil. Then, dredge the catfish in the flour to coat and discard the excess.
5. Now dip the coated catfish in the beaten egg and sprinkle breadcrumbs on top of it, covering the catfish evenly.

6. Add the catfish in the air fryer basket and spray some cooking oil.

7. Set the air fryer at 400°F and cook for 8 minutes until the fish gets tender. Halfway through the cooking, flip the fish.

8. Sprinkle them with pepper and salt as desired. In a medium bowl, whisk together the mayonnaise, relish, dill, sugar & vinegar to make the tartar sauce.

9. Serve hot with lemon wedges and tartar sauce.

Nutritional Information:

Calories 416, Carbohydrates: 31g, Fat 18g, Protein: 33g, Cholesterol 52mg, Sodium: 677mg, Potassium: 71mg, Sugars: 8g, Saturated fat: 3.5g, Calcium: 39mg.

White Fish

Preparation time: 5 minutes

Cooking time: 10 minutes

Total time: 15 minutes

Servings: 2

Ingredients:

- 12 ounces tilapia fillets
- ½ tsp. lemon pepper seasoning.
- ½ tsp. black pepper, crushed
- 1 lemon
- ¼ cup chopped parsley
- ½ tsp. salt
- ½ ground black pepper
- ½ tsp. garlic powder
- ½ tsp. onion powder
- Olive spray

Cooking Instructions:

1. Cut the lemon into wedges and set aside. Set the air fryer to 360°F and preheat for 5 minutes.
2. Clean and rinse the fish fillets. Pat dry the fillets.
3. Combine together the garlic powder, onion powder, lemon pepper, ground black pepper, garlic powder, and salt in a medium bowl.
4. Spray some olive oil on the fillets. Rub the spice mix on both sides of the fish fillet. Spread a perforated parchment paper in the air fryer basket.
5. Spray some olive oil over it. Add the seasoned fillet on the parchment paper in the air fryer basket and place some wedges on the side.
6. Cook the fillet for 12 minutes until you can flake the fish with a fork. Halfway through the cooking flip the fillets.
7. Serve with chopped parsley and toasted wedges.

Nutritional Information:

Calories: 150, Total fat: 1.7g, Saturated fat: 0.7g, Cholesterol: 83mg, Sodium: 654mg, Total carbs: 2g, Dietary fiber: 0.5g, Total sugars: 0.5g, Protein: 32.4g, Calcium: 46mg, Potassium: 62mg.

Crispy Fish Fillets

Preparation time: 15 minutes

Cooking time: 15 minutes

Total time: 30 minutes

Servings: 8

Ingredients:

- 28 ounces fish fillets
- ½ tsp. paprika
- ¼ tsp. chili powder, dry
- 1 cup bread crumbs
- ½ tsp. Salt
- 1 tsp. olive oil
- ¼ tsp. onion Powder
- ¼ tsp. garlic powder
- ¼ tsp. ground black pepper

Cooking Instructions:

1. If you're using frozen fillets, defrost it and sprinkle with some olive oil. Give everything a good mix to coat evenly.

2. In a medium bowl, mix together the chili powder, paprika, onion powder, garlic powder, black pepper powder, and salt with the bread crumbs.

3. Take the coated fillets and dip them in the mixing bowl. Coat every fillet in the bread crumbs evenly.

4. Place the fillets in the Air fryer basket. Set the air fryer to 390°F and cook the fillets for at least 12-15 minutes.

5. Open the fryer after 8 minutes and flip the fish fillets to continue cooking for the remaining period.

6. Garnish it with lemon slices or tomatoes. Serve hot and enjoy!

Nutritional Information:

Calories 153, Carbohydrates: 11g, fat 3g, Protein: 21g, Cholesterol 50mg, Sodium: 269mg, Potassium: 302mg, Sugars: 1g, Saturated fat: 2.0g, Calcium: 10mg.

Fish Sticks

Preparation time: 10 minutes

Cooking time: 30 minutes

Total time: 40 minutes

Servings: 2

Ingredients:

- 1-pound codfish
- 2 eggs
- 1 tsp. onion powder
- ½ tsp. dill
- 1 tsp. ground black pepper
- 2 tbsp. avocado oil
- ½ tsp. mustard powder
- 1 tsp. salt
- ½ cup tapioca starch
- 1 cup almond flour
- Avocado oil spray

Cooking Instructions:

1. Rinse the fish and pat dry. Coat the fish with ground pepper and salt.
2. Cut the fish into bite size, approximately 2 inches length, and half-inch thickness. Add the tapioca starch in a medium-size bowl.
3. In a separate bowl, beat the eggs. In a large bowl, combine together the dill, almond flour, pepper, salt, mustard powder, and onion powder.
4. Set the air temperature to 390°F and preheat. Dredge the stick size fish in the tapioca starch and sink into the beaten egg.
5. Discard any excess liquid and dredge the fish into the flour mixture. Repeat the procedure for the rest of the fish pieces.
6. Brush little quantity of avocado oil on the air fryer basket. Add the seasoned fish in the air fryer basket and spray with avocado cooking oil.
7. Do not overcrowd the cooking basket. Cook the seasoned fish for 11 minutes.
8. Halfway through the cooking, gently flip the fish.
9. Serve with your desired sauce and enjoy!

Nutritional Information:

Calories: 231, Total fat: 6.6g, Saturated fat: 1.8g, Cholesterol: 164mg, Sodium: 1228mg, Total carbs: 37.1g, Dietary fiber: 1.5g, Total sugars: 2.2g, Protein: 6.3g, Calcium: 50mg, Potassium: 146mg.

Salt and Pepper Shrimp

Preparation time: 10 minutes

Cooking time: 10 minutes

Total time: 20 minutes

Servings: 4

Ingredients:

- 1-pound shrimp
- 3 tbsp. rice flour
- 2 tsp. ground peppercorns
- 2 tsp. ground black peppercorns
- 1 tsp. sugar
- 1 teaspoon salt
- 2 tablespoons oil
- Cooking spray

Cooking Instructions:

1. In a saucepan, add the Sichuan peppercorns and black peppercorns and roast on medium-low temperature for about 2 minutes.
2. Let to cool for a couple of minutes after roasting. Add some salt to it and crush it to make a fine powder.
3. Peel, devein, and rinse the shrimps. Add the shrimps in a large bowl. Add the rice flour, spices, and oil onto the shrimps and stir to combine.
4. Spray some cooking oil on the air fryer basket. Add the shrimps onto the air fryer basket without overcrowding. Spray some cooking oil.
5. Set the temperature of the air fryer to 330°F and cook for 10 minutes.
6. Toss the air fryer halfway through the cooking.
7. Serve hot and enjoy!

Nutritional Information:

Calories: 178, Total fat: 8g, Saturated fat: 1g, Carbohydrates: 9g, Protein: 16g, Cholesterol: 143mg, Sodium: 1224mg, Dietary fiber: 1g, Potassium: 187mg, Sugars: 1g, Calcium: 81mg, Iron: 0.7mg

Cheese Potato Wedges

Preparation time: 15 minutes

Cooking time: 16 minutes

Total time: 31 minutes

Servings: 4

Ingredients:

- 1-pound potatoes
- ½ tsp. garlic powder
- 15 raw cashews
- ½ tsp. turmeric, ground
- ½ tsp. paprika
- 2 tbsp. nutritional yeast
- 1 tsp. fresh lemon juice
- 5 tbsp. water Cooking spray
- 1 tsp. extra virgin olive oil
- 1 tsp. kosher salt
- 1 tsp. black pepper, ground

Cooking Instructions:

1. Wash the potatoes and cut them into halves and then lengthwise.
2. Soak in the water for 10 minutes to remove the excess starch. Pat the potatoes dry with a paper towel and add them in a medium bowl.
3. Set the air fryer temperature to 400°F and preheat for 5 minutes.
4. Add some oil, garlic powder, and pepper to the potatoes and give everything a good mix to coat.
5. Add the potatoes in the air fryer basket and drizzle with some cooking oil. Cook for 16 minutes. Shake the air fryer basket and tossing the potatoes halfway to ensure even cooking.
6. In a separate bowl, add together the turmeric, cashews, yeast, paprika, and lemon juice and transfer it to the blender.
7. Blend it on slow speed until it turns to a smooth paste with loose consistency. Add a little water to maintain the consistency if desired.

8. Once the cooking time over, place them on a parchment paper or an air fryer safe pan. Drizzle the blended cheese sauce over the potatoes wedges.

9. Add them in the air fryer and cook for additional 2 minutes. Allow it to cool for a couple of minutes before serving.

10. Serve and enjoy!

Nutritional Information:

Calories 183, Carbohydrates: 27g, Total fat: 6.2g, Protein: 7g, Saturated fat: 1.1g, Trans fat: 0g, Cholesterol: 0mg, Sodium: 867mg, Sugars: 2g

Cauliflower Chickpea Tacos

Preparation time: 10 minutes

Cooking time: 20 minutes

Total time: 30 minutes

Servings: 4

Ingredients:

- 1 cauliflower, cut in bite-sized florets
- 2 tbsp. taco seasoning
- 8 small tortillas
- 2 avocados, sliced
- ½ cabbage, shredded
- 3 tsp. coconut yogurt
- 1 can (19 ounces) of chickpeas
- 2 tbsp. olive oil

Cooking Instructions:

1. Set the air fryer to 390°F and preheat for 5 minutes.
2. Combine together the cauliflower, chickpea, along with olive oil and taco seasoning in a medium bowl.
3. Add the mixture in the air fryer basket and cook for 20 minutes.
4. Stir the ingredients occasionally for even cooking.
5. Remove the basket when the cauliflower turns golden brown.
6. Serve with avocado slices, cabbage, and coconut yogurt.

Nutritional Information:

Calories: 1047, Total fat: 35.4g, Saturated fat: 5.4g, Trans fat: 0g, Cholesterol: 0mg, Sodium: 1050mg, Total carbs: 150g, Dietary fiber: 28g, Sugars: 21g, Protein: 39g

Lemon Tofu

Preparation time: 15 minutes

Cooking time: 25 minutes

Total time: 40 minutes

Servings: 4

Ingredients:

- 1 tsp. lemon zest
- 3 tsp. lemon juice
- ½ cup of water
- 2 tbsp. sugar, organic
- 2 tsp. cornstarch
- 1-pound tofu, extra-firm, drained and pressed
- 1 tbsp. tamari
- 1 tbsp. cornstarch

Cooking Instructions:

1. Cut the Tofu with a knife into bite-size pieces
2. Place these cubes in a plastic Ziploc bag and add tamari over it. Seal the bag and shake the bag well to coat the tamari on the Tofu.
3. Add 1 tbsp. of cornstarch to the bag and shake to coat thoroughly. Set aside for about 15 minutes for a better marinade effect.
4. In a medium bowl, mix all the other sauces for later use. Place the Tofu in the air fryer basket in a single layer, do not overlap.
5. Cook the Tofu at 390°F for 10 minutes and shake the basket after 5 minutes for even cooking.
6. Repeat the same procedure for the remaining batches of Tofu. Give the sauce a good stir and drizzle over the Tofu.
7. Serve with rice and steamed vegetables and enjoy!

Nutritional Information:

Calories 112, Carbohydrates: 13g, fat 3g, Protein: 8, Sodium: 294 mg, Potassium: 250mg, Sugars: 8g, Calcium: 36mg

Potato Chips

Preparation time: 5 minutes

Cooking time: 15 minutes

Total time: 20 minutes

Servings: 4

Ingredients:

- 1 cooking spray

- 2 tsp. of sea salt

- 1 russet potato, large, thinly sliced

Cooking Instructions:

1. Peel and wash the potatoes with clean water. Slice it thinly and pat dry with a paper towel.

2. Sprinkle the air fryer basket with some cooking oil and add the potatoes one at a time, without overlapping in the basket.

3. You can cook the potatoes in batches. Spray the cooking oil over the potatoes.

4. Set the air fryer temperature at 450°F. Cook for 15 minutes or until the edges turn golden brown and crispy.

5. Immediately the edges begin to turn dark brown and the middle part of the chips is lighter, remove them from the air fryer.

6. Transfer it to a counter to crisp and cool. Serve and enjoy!

Nutritional Information:

Calories 74.3, Carbohydrates: 17.6g, fat 0g, Protein: 2g, Cholesterol 0mg, Sodium: 290.7mg, Potassium: 419mg, Sugars: 0.7g, Saturated fat: 0g

Avocado Egg Rolls

Preparation time: 20 minutes

Cooking time: 25 minutes

Total time: 45 minutes

Servings: 5

Ingredients:

Avocado Egg Rolls:

- 1½ avocadoes
- ¼ tsp. of ground black pepper
- ¼ garlic powder
- 4 full-size egg roll wrappers
- ½ tsp. kosher salt
- ½ tsp. chili powder
- Vegetable cooking spray
- ¼ cup red onion, diced
- ¼ cup chopped cilantro
- 2 tbsp. tomatoes, sun-dried
- 1 tbsp. lime juice

Avocado Dip:

- 1 avocado
- ¼ tsp. kosher salt
- ¼ tsp. ground black pepper
- ¼ tsp. cayenne pepper
- 2 tbsp. light sour cream
- 2 tsp. lime juice
- 1 tbsp. Greek yogurt, non-fat

Cooking Instructions:

1. Wash the avocadoes and pat dry with a paper towel. Dice the avocadoes.
2. Add together the lime juice, pepper, diced avocado, red onion, cilantro, sun-dried tomatoes, chili powder, salt, garlic powder, and pepper in a medium bowl.
3. Give the mixture a good stir to combine. Divide the mixture into 4 equal portions.

4. Add a quarter of the avocado egg roll mixture into the center of 4 egg roll wrappers. Ensure that the wrapper is placed in a triangular shape.

5. Brush the 4 edges of the wrapper with water.

6. From the bottom side, start folding the wrapper over the filling towards the upper side. Followed by, fold each side over the other.

7. The moisture edges of the wrapper will enable the edges to stick firmly.

8. Repeat the procedure with the remaining wrappers. Spritz cooking oil over the rolls. Set the air fryer temperature to 400°F and preheat for 3 minutes.

9. Spray the air fryer basket with some cooking oil and add the rolls in it.

10. Set the timer for 8 minutes and start cooking. Flip the egg rolls after 4 minutes and continue cooking spritzing some cooking oil.

11. While cooking the rolls, prepare the dipping sauce.

12. Add all the sauce ingredients in a food processor and pulse it.

13. Serve the avocado egg rolls with avocado dipping.

Nutritional Information:

Calories: 126, Carbs: 13.5g, Protein: 2.8g, Total fat: 7.4g, Saturated fat: 1g, Cholesterol: 2.8mg, Sodium: 206mg, Potassium: 270mg, Fiber: 3.7g, Sugar: 1.8g, Calcium: 31mg

Sushi Rolls

Preparation time: 1 hour 10 minutes

Cooking time: 10 minutes

Total time: 1 hour 20 minutes

Servings: 3

Ingredients:

- 1 ½ cups kale
- 1 tbsp. sesame seeds, toasted
- 1½ cup cooled pressure-cooked sushi rice
- 3 sheets of sushi nori
- ½ avocado, sliced
- 6 tbsp. mayonnaise
- 1 tsp. sriracha sauce
- 15 tbsp. panko bread crumbs
- ½ tsp. rice vinegar
- ¾ tsp. sesame oil, toasted
- ⅛ tsp. garlic powder
- ¼ tsp. ginger, ground
- ¾ tsp. soy sauce

Cooking Instructions:

1. Wash the kale, remove the ribs, pat dry, and coarsely slice.
2. Combine together the kale, sesame oil, vinegar, ginger, garlic powder, and soy sauce in a medium bowl.
3. Rub the kale with your hand until it wilts and turns a brighter green. Add some sesame seeds and set aside.
4. Place the nori sheet on your working table to start the sushi rolls. With lightly damp hand, grab a handful of rice and spread over the nori sheet.
5. Have a thin layer of rice over the sheet. Leave about ½ inch of naked seaweed at the edge to use as a flap to roll the sushi.
6. Add 2-3 tbsp. of kale salad on the opposite side of the naked seaweed. Add some avocado slices over them and make your filling.
7. When the filling process is over, roll the sushi by pressing it down gently from the end. Use the naked portion of the seaweed to seal the sushi roll.

8. Repeat the same procedure for the remaining batches of sushi rolls.

9. To make the sriracha sauce, whisk together the mayonnaise and sriracha in a separate bowl. Keep checking the spice level as desired.

10. Then, pour the panko breadcrumbs in a medium bowl. Take the sushi roll one at a time and dredge it in the sriracha sauce and then dip in the panko breadcrumbs mixture.

11. Dab it well to ensure that the sushi is well coated with panko. Repeat the same procedure with other rolls.

12. Transfer the rolls in the air fryer basket. Set the air fryer 390°F for 10 minutes. Shake the air fryer basket after 5 minutes.

13. Allow it to cool for a couple of minutes before serving.

14. Cut it into 6-8 pieces as required and serve with soy sauce dipping.

15. Serve immediately and enjoy!

Nutritional Information:

Calories: 832, Total fat: 26g, Saturated fat: 3.6g, Trans fat: 0.1g, Cholesterol: 0mg, Sodium: 1424mg, Total carbs: 126g, Dietary fiber: 10g, Sugars: 19g, Protein: 24g

Cheese Samosa

Preparation time: 30 minutes

Cooking time: 12 minutes

Total time: 42 minutes

Servings: 20

Ingredients:

For the Cheese:

- 5 tbsp. tapioca starch
- ¾ tsp. sea salt
- 1 tsp. apple cider vinegar
- 1¼ cup of water
- 8-10 raw cashews, pre-boiled for 10 minutes
- 3 tbsp. nutritional yeast

For the Samboosa:

- 1 tbsp. olive oil
- ½ cup of water
- 1 Packet samosa pastry sheets

Cooking Instructions:

1. Add the cheese ingredients in a blender and blend until smooth. Pour the blended mixture in a small saucepan and bring to medium heat.
2. Stir the blended ingredients frequently while cooking. Cook for about 5 minutes, while stirring continuously to become firm.
3. Store this mixture in a glass container and refrigerate for about 30 minutes before using. Add the samosa pastry vertically on a flat surface and sprinkle with a dash of water using a brush, to stick the edges smoothly.
4. On the right corner of the pastry sheet, add the cheese mixture and fold the pastry from the bottom to create a triangle shape.
5. Fold the right-side pointing downward to create a perfect triangle parcel and seal the ends with slightly moistening your hand.
6. Repeat the same procedure for the remaining batches of pastry sheet.
7. To cook the samboosa, brush it with olive oil on each of the sides. Add the parcels in the air fryer one at a time, avoiding overlapping.
8. Set the air fryer temperature to 390°F. Cook for about 10 minutes.

9. Flip the samboosa midway through the cooking and continue cooking until it turns brown.

10. Serve with your desired sauce and enjoy!

Nutritional Information:

Calories: 55, Total fat: 2.5g, Trans fat: 0.2g, Cholesterol: 1mg, Sodium: 188mg, Total carbs: 7g, Dietary fiber: 0g, Sugars: 2g, Protein: 1g

Kale and Potato Nuggets

Preparation time: 10 minutes

Cooking time: 30 minutes

Total time: 40 minutes

Servings: 4

Ingredients:

- 2 potatoes, finely chopped
- 4 cup kale, chopped
- 10 tbsp. almond milk
- ¼ tsp. of sea salt
- ¼ tsp. ground black pepper
- 1 tsp. olive oil
- 1 garlic clove, minced
- Cooking spray

Cooking Instructions:

1. In a medium saucepan, add the potatoes and cook for about 30 minutes until they become tender.

2. Add some oil into a large skillet and bring to medium-high heat. When the oil is hot, add garlic into it. Cook the garlic until it turns golden.

3. Add the kale and sauté for another 2-3 minutes. Once the kale gets wilted, transfer it to a container to cool for a couple of minutes.

4. Drain the potatoes from the boiling water and place in a medium bowl. Add milk, pepper, salt, and mash the potato with a fork or a masher.

5. Combine this mixture with the cooked kale. Set the air fryer to 390°F and preheat for 5 minutes.

6. With the mashed potato and kale mixture, make 1-inch nugget rolls. Add the nuggets in the air fryer basket and drizzle some cooking oil.

7. Cook the rolls for 15 minutes until they turn golden brown. Flip the nuggets, halfway through the cooking and drizzle some cooking oil.

8. Serve hot along with dipping.

Nutritional Information:

Calories: 185, Total carbs: 36g, Dietary fiber: 5g, Sugars: 4g, Total fat: 2.7g, Saturated fat: 0.9g, Trans fat: 0g, Cholesterol: 4mg, Sodium: 179mg, Protein: 6g.

Tofu Cauliflower

Preparation time: 5 minutes

Cooking time: 24 minutes

Total time: 29 minutes

Servings: 4

Ingredients:

- 2 tsp. avocado oil
- 3 tbsp. nutritional yeast
- ¼ tsp. of sea salt
- 1 tbsp. cornstarch
- 1 head cauliflower, medium size
- 3 tbsp. red hot sauce
- 1½ tsp. maple syrup

Cooking Instructions:

1. Cut the cauliflower to 1½ inch florets. Set the Air Fryer at 360°F.
2. In a medium bowl, add together all the ingredients, except for the cauliflower florets. Whisk the ingredients to combine thoroughly.
3. Add the cauliflower at the end and ensure that they are coated. Add half of the cauliflower in the air fryer without oil and cook for about 14 minutes.
4. Shake the air fryer basket regularly. Repeat the procedure with the second batch of cauliflower as well.
5. Serve hot and enjoy!

Nutritional Information:

Calories: 78, Total fat: 2.6g, Saturated fat: 0.4g, Tans fat: 0g, Cholesterol: 0mg, Sodium: 569mg, Total carbs: 10g, Dietary fiber: 2g, Sugars:3g, Protein: 5g

Ravoili

Preparation time: 8 minutes

Cooking time: 23 minutes

Total time: 31 minutes

Servings: 4

Ingredients:

- 10 tbsp. panko breadcrumbs
- 1 tsp. garlic powder
- 1 tsp. salt
- 1 tsp. pepper
- 10 tbsp. of aquafaba
- 8 ounces of frozen vegan ravioli
- 5 tbsp. marinara
- 1 cooking spray, spritz
- 2 tsp. nutritional yeast
- 1 tsp. basil, dried
- 1 tsp. oregano, dried

Cooking Instructions:

1. Add together the nutritional yeast, panko bread crumbs, dried basil, dried oregano, salt, pepper, garlic powder in a medium bowl.
2. Mix the ingredients to form a dry mixture. In a separate bowl, pour the aquafaba. Dip the ravioli pieces in the aquafaba, shake away the excess.
3. Dredge it in the bread crumb mixture. Drizzle the air fryer basket with some cooking oil and add the ravioli without overlapping.
4. Spray the cooking spray over the ravioli. Set the air fryer at 390°F and cook the ravioli for 6 minutes.
5. Carefully flip the ravioli and cook for additional 2 minutes. After cooking, transfer the ravioli to a serving plate.
6. Serve hot with the marinara as a dipping.

Nutritional Information:

Calories 150, Carbohydrates: 27g, Protein: 5g, Sodium: 411mg, Potassium: 145mg, Sugars: 1g, Calcium: 36mg

Buffalo Cauliflower Bite

Preparation time: 10 minutes

Cooking time: 20 minutes

Total time: 30 minutes

Servings: 4

Ingredients:

- 4 cups, florets of cauliflower, cut into 1" size
- ½ teaspoon, grated garlic clove
- 1 Egg white
- ¼ cup sour cream low fat
- 1 teaspoon red wine vinegar
- ¼ teaspoon ground black pepper
- 1 tablespoon, grated blue cheese
- ¾ cup breadcrumbs
- 2 tablespoons hot sauce
- 3 tablespoons no salt ketchup
- Cooking spray

Cooking Instructions:

1. In a medium bowl, combine together the ketchup, hot sauce and beaten egg white. Add the breadcrumbs on another plate.
2. Dip the cauliflower florets in the ketchup mixture and then dredge in the breadcrumbs till it gets a thick coating.
3. Place a baking sheet in the air fryer basket. Add the coated cauliflower florets on the baking sheet. Spray some cooking oil over it.
4. Set the air fryer at 320°F and bake for 20 minutes. Cook in batches to avoid overcrowding the air fryer basket.
5. Shake the air fryer basket midway through the cooking for even cooking. Cook until it becomes golden brown.
6. In a medium bowl, combine together the sour cream, garlic, blue cheese, red wine vinegar, and pepper to make the sauce.
7. Serve fried cauliflower along with the sauce.

Nutritional Information:

Calories:125, Carbs:17g, Fat: 4, Saturated fat: 2g, Protein: 5g, Dietary fiber: 1g, Sugars: 6g, Sodium: 255mg

Calzones

Preparation time: 15 minutes

Cooking time: 20 minutes

Total time: 35 minutes

Servings: 2

Ingredients:

- 6 ounces whole-wheat pizza dough, fresh.
- ⅓ cup shredded chicken breast
- 3 cups baby spinach leaves
- ¼ cup finely chopped red onions
- 1 teaspoon olive oil
- ⅓ cup low sodium Marinara sauce
- Cooking spray

Cooking Instructions:

1. Add the olive oil into a medium-size nonstick skillet and bring to medium heat. Once the skillet becomes hot, add onion and sauté for about 4 minutes.
2. Add the spinach and cook for about 2 minutes to get the leaves wilted. Turn off the heat and add shredded chicken and sauce.
3. Divide the dough into 4 portions. On your working table, spread some flour and roll the dough into a 6-inch circle.
4. Place some spinach mixture over half a portion of the dough circle. Add little cheese over the spinach mixture.
5. Fold the non-filled portion over the filled-up portion like a half-moon. Crimp edges by pressing with a fork. Spray the calzones with some cooking oil.
6. Set the air fryer temperature to 325°F. Spray some cooking oil on the air fryer basket and add the calzones in the basket.
7. Place the basket in the air fryer and bake for 12 minutes. After 12 minutes, turn the calzones and cooking additional 8 minutes.
8. Serve hot along with ketchup.

Nutritional Information:

Calories: 348, Fat: 12g, Saturated fat: 3g, Protein: 21g, Carbohydrate: 44g, Dietary fiber: 5g, Sugars: 3g, Sodium: 710mg

Sweet Potato Tots

Preparation time: 10 minutes

Cooking time: 42 minutes

Total time: 52 minutes

Servings: 4

Ingredients:

- 2 sweet potatoes, small
- 1 tablespoon potato starch
- ¾ cup salt less ketchup
- ⅛ teaspoon ground garlic
- 1¼ teaspoon kosher salt
- Cooking spray

Cooking Instructions:

1. Add the sweet potatoes in a saucepan and boil for about 15 minutes. Allow it to cool for a couple of minutes and peel off the skin.
2. Grate potatoes using a box grater that has larger holes. Add the grated potatoes in a mixing bowl, add potato starch, garlic powder, and a teaspoon of salt.
3. Toss the grated potatoes to this mixture and make a tot shaped cylinders of one inch. Spray some cooking on the air fryer basket.
4. Place the tots in a single layer in the basket and avoid overcrowding. Spray some cooking oil over the tots. Cook at 400°F until it becomes brown for 15 minutes.
5. Halfway through the cooking, turn the tots and cook for additional 12 minutes. Sprinkle little salt while serving.
6. Serve hot with ketchup and enjoy!

Nutritional Information:

Calories: 50, Total fat: 0.1g, Saturated fat: 0g, Cholesterol: 0mg, Sodium: 1605mg, Total carbs: 11.4g, Dietary fiber: 1.7g, Total sugars: 0.9g, Protein: 1.2g, Calcium: 7mg, Potassium: 287mg

Churros

Preparation time: 20 minutes

Cooking time: 30minutes

Total time: 50 minutes

Servings: 12

Ingredients:

- 4 ounces bittersweet baking chocolate, grated.
- ½ cup all-purpose flour
- ¼ tsp. kosher salt
- ¼ cup+2 tbsp. unsalted butter
- ½ cup of water
- 2 large eggs
- ⅓ granulated sugar
- 2 tsp. ground cinnamon
- 2 tbsp. vanilla
- 3 tbsp. heavy cream

Cooking Instructions:

1. Add water and ¼ of the butter in a small saucepan. Bring the pan to a boil on medium-high temperature until the butter starts to melt.
2. Add the flour little by little and stir continuously with a spatula without any lumps. Continue this process until the dough becomes thick.
3. Once the dough becomes thick, transfer it to a bowl. Continue stirring and let it cool and set aside. Add the eggs one by one and stir continuously until smooth.
4. Transfer the mixture to a piping bag with a star tip. Allow it to cool for a couple of minutes. Pipe into 3 inches long pieces in one layer into the air fryer basket.
5. Set the air fryer temperature at 380°F and cook for 10 minutes until it turns golden brown. Repeat the same procedure for the remaining dough.
6. In another bowl, mix sugar and cinnamon. Brush the cooked churros with melted butter and rollover sugar mixture to get a fine coating.
7. Now let us prepare the chocolate cream. Add the chocolate and cream in a microwave-safe bowl.
8. Microwave it on high to get a smooth and melted texture for about half an hour. Stir smoothly after 15 seconds.

9. Serve the churros with the chocolate sauce.

Calories: 173, Fat: 11g, Saturated fat: 7g, Protein: 3g, Carbs: 12g, Dietary fiber: 1g, Sugars: 7g, Sodium: 55mg.

Loaded Potatoes

Preparation time: 10 minutes

Cooking time: 32 minutes

Total time: 42 minutes

Servings: 2

Ingredients:

- 11 ounces baby potatoes
- 2 bacons, crushed
- 1 tsp. olive oil
- 1½ tbsp. fresh chives chopped
- ½ ounce low-fat cheddar cheese, grated
- 2 tbsp. sour cream, low fat
- ⅛ tsp. kosher salt

Cooking Instructions:

1. In a nonstick pan, toss the potatoes with oil for a coating.
2. Add the potatoes in the air fryer basket. Set the air fryer at 350°F to cook for 25 minutes until it becomes tender, stirring continuously.
3. In a medium-size skillet, add the bacon and cook for 7 minutes, until it becomes crispy. Remove it from the heat and allow to cool for a couple of minutes.
4. Crumble the bacon. Transfer the potatoes into a serving plate and slightly crush it to split. Sprinkle crushed bacon over the crushed potatoes.
5. Garnish with chives, cheese, and sour cream, and salt.
6. Serve hot with ketchup.

Nutritional Information:

Calories: 199, Total fat: 7g, Saturated fat: 3g, Protein: 7g, Carbs: 26g, Dietary fiber: 4g, Sugars: 3g, Sodium: 287mg.

Spicy Chicken Wing Drumettes

Preparation time: 15 minutes

Cooking time: 25 minutes

Total time: 40 minutes

Servings: 2

Ingredients:

- 10 chicken drumettes
- ¼ cup of rice vinegar
- 3 tbsp. honey
- 1 tbsp. sesame oil, toasted
- 1 tbsp. soy sauce, low-sodium
- 2 tbsp. unsalted chicken stock
- 1 tbsp. sesame oil
- ⅛ tsp. ground red pepper
- 1 clove garlic, minced
- 2 tbsp. roasted peanuts, unsalted
- ⅛ tsp. salt
- 1 tbsp. fresh chives, finely chopped
- Cooking spray

Cooking Instructions:

1. Wash the chicken and pat dry with a paper towel. Spray some cooking oil and place it in the air fryer cooking basket.
2. Set the air fryer at 400°F and cook for 30 minutes. Turn the chicken midway for even cooking.
6. In a medium skillet, add together the soy sauce, chicken stock, vinegar, sesame oil, garlic, red pepper, salt and give everything a good stir to combine.
7. Heat the ingredients in low-medium temperature, until it becomes thick for about 6 minutes. Add the fried chicken into the sauce.
8. Pour honey over it and toss. Garnish with chopped chives and roasted peanuts.
9. Serve immediately and enjoy!

Nutritional Information:

Calories: 6699, Total fat: 177.8g, Saturated fat: 42.2g, Cholesterol: 3721mg, Sodium: 4574mg, Total carbs: 33g, Dietary fiber: 1g, Sugars: 22g, Protein: 11368g

Empanadas

Preparation time: 15 minutes

Cooking time: 30 minutes

Total time: 45 minutes

Servings: 2

Ingredients:

- 3 ounces ground lean beef
- ¼ cup white onion, finely chopped
- 3 ounces mushrooms, finely chopped
- ½ cup tomatoes, chopped
- 6 olives, pitted
- 2 teaspoons, minced garlic
- 1 tablespoon olive oil
- ¼ teaspoon paprika
- ¼ teaspoon cumin powder
- ⅛ teaspoon cinnamon powder
- 1 egg, large
- 8 square gyoza wrappers

Cooking Instructions:

1. Add the oil in a large skillet and bring to low-medium heat. Add onion, beef and cook for about 3 minutes, until the beef crumbles and turns brown.
2. Add the mushrooms and continue stirring for additional 2 minutes. Add together the cumin powder, olives, cumin powder, and garlic.
3. Continue cooking until the mushrooms become tender for about 4 minutes. Add the tomatoes and sauté for 2 minutes.
4. After cooking, transfer it to a bowl and allow to cool for a couple of minutes.
5. In a small bowl beat the egg. Then, spread the wrappers on the working table.
6. Add 1½ tablespoons of fillers at the center of the wrapper. Brush the tips of the wrapper with beaten egg. Fold the wrapper and crimp the edges.
7. Fill all the wrappers and crimp. Set the air fryer to 400°F. Add the empanadas in the air fryer basket and cook for 7 minutes.
8. Flip halfway and continue cooking. Serve hot.

Nutritional Information:

Calories: 393, Total fat: 19.2g, Saturated fat: 4.5g, Cholesterol: 347mg, Sodium: 256mg, Total carbs: 40g, Dietary fiber: 6g, Sugars: 3g, Protein: 21g

Sweet Potato Chips

Preparation time: 25 minutes

Cooking time: 15 minutes

Total time: 40 minutes

Servings: 4

Ingredients:

- 1 large sweet potato.
- ¼ tsp. ground black pepper
- ¼ tsp. salt
- 1 tbsp. canola oil
- 1 tsp. rosemary, chopped
- Cooking spray

Cooking Instructions:

1. Wash and peel the potato. Slice the potato into thin chips.
2. In a medium bowl, add the potatoes and soak for about 20 minutes. Drain by using a collator and keep the chips dry.
3. Add pepper, rosemary, black pepper and toss. Spray the air fryer basket with some cooking oil.
4. Add the potato chips into the basket. Spray some cooking oil onto it.
5. Set the temperature at 350°F and cook for 15 minutes.
6. Halfway of cooking just toss the potatoes and spray some cooking oil.
7. After cooking, transfer to a serving bowl.
8. Serve crisp and enjoy!

Nutritional Information:

Calories: 73, Total fat: 0.3g, Cholesterol: 0mg, Sodium: 162mg, Total carbs: 10g, Dietary fiber: 2g, Sugars: 3g, Protein: 1g

Chicken Wings

Preparation time: 10 minutes

Cooking time: 29 minutes

Total time: 39 minutes

Servings: 2

Ingredients:

- 10 chicken wings
- ½ tsp. corn starch
- 2 tsp. honey
- 1 tbsp. soy sauce, low-sodium
- 1 tsp. ground chili paste
- 1 tsp. garlic minced
- ½ tsp. minced ginger
- ¼ tsp. salt
- 1 tsp. lime juice
- 2 tbsp. scallions, chopped
- Cooking spray

Cooking Instructions:

1. Wash the chicken and pat dry with a paper towel. Spray some cooking oil onto it. Add the chicken wings in the air fryer basket without overlapping.
2. Set the air fryer at 400°F and cook for 25 minutes. Flip the drumettes after 10-15 minutes and continue cooking.
3. In a medium skillet combine ginger, chili paste, honey, garlic, salt, and lime juice. Slow heat by stirring for 3-4 minutes, until it starts to bubble.
4. Add the chicken into it and pour soy sauce. Toss everything to combine. Garnish with scallions before serving.
5. Serve and enjoy!

Nutritional Information:

Calories: 5351, Total fat: 130.5g, Saturated fat: 32.3g, Cholesterol: 3101mg, Sodium: 4029mg, Total carbs: 10g, Dietary fiber: 1g, Sugars: 8g, Protein: 971g.

Italian-Style Meatballs

Preparation time: 10 minutes

Cooking time: 35 minutes

Total time: 45 minutes

Servings: 12

Ingredients:

- 12 ounces ground lean beef
- 5 ounces turkey sausages
- 2 tbsp. olive oil
- 2 tbsp. whole milk
- 2 tbsp. shallot, minced
- 1 tbsp. cloves minced garlic
- ¼ cup bread crumbs
- 1 egg large
- 1 tbsp. finely chopped fresh thyme
- 1 tbsp. rosemary, fresh
- ¼ cup parsley, fresh, chopped
- 1 tbsp. Dijon mustard
- ½ tsp. salt

Cooking Instructions:

1. Set the air fryer at 400°F and preheat. In a large nonstick skillet, add some oil and bring to medium-high heat.
2. Add the shallot into the skillet and give everything a good stir to soften for about 4 minutes. After that, add garlic and cook for about 1 minute.
3. In a large bowl, mix together the breadcrumbs and milk. Allow it to sit for about 5 minutes. Add the cooked shallot and garlic into the bread crumb mixture.
4. In a medium bowl, beat the egg. Add turkey sausages, beef, beaten egg, rosemary, parsley, mustard, thyme, and salt. Give everything a good stir.
5. Scoop out the mixture and make small meatballs into 1½-inch size. Spread a parchment paper in the air fryer basket.
6. Add the meatballs on the parchment paper in the air fryer basket. Cook the meatballs for 12 minutes.
7. Flip the meatballs midway so that the balls can have even cooking.

8. Serve along with noodles, pasta or rice.

Nutritional Information:

Calories: 119, Total fat: 7.2g, Saturated fat: 2.1g, Cholesterol: 48mg, Sodium: 221mg, Total carbs: 3g, Dietary fiber: 0g, Sugars: 1g, Protein: 10g

CHAPTER SEVEN
DESSERT RECIPES
Chocolate Chip Cookies

Preparation time: 15 minutes

Cooking time: 10 minutes

Total time: 25 minutes

Servings: 8

Ingredients:

- ½ cup of sugar
- 1 tsp. vanilla
- 1½ cup all-purpose flour
- 1 cup of chocolate chips
- ½ cup brown sugar
- ½ cup butter kept in room temperature
- 1 egg
- ½ tsp. baking soda
- ¼ tsp. salt

Cooking Instructions:

1. Set the air fryer to 350°F and preheat. Grease the baking tray with butter.
2. In a medium bowl, combine together the sugar, butter, and brown sugar.
3. Crack the egg into it and blend. Add salt, baking soda, and all-purpose flour.
4. Blend and mix the ingredients. Then, add the chocolate chips and combine thoroughly with the mixture.
5. Scoop the dough and press on the oiled baking tray.
6. Start baking for 12 minutes until it becomes golden brown at the edges.
7. Using a butter knife cut into 8 pieces.
8. Serve warm and enjoy!

Nutritional Information:

Calories: 517, Total fat: 7.7g, Saturated fat: 4.7g, Cholesterol: 26mg, Sodium: 182mg, Total carbs: 99.6mg, Dietary fiber: 3g, Protein: 11.2g, Total sugars: 32.5g, Calcium: 63mg, Potassium: 190mg.

Caramel Apple Cracker

Preparation time: 5 minutes

Cooking time: 14 minutes

Total time: 19 minutes

Servings: 4

Ingredients:

- 1 green apple
- 4 marshmallows
- 8 graham cracker squares
- 4 teaspoons caramel sauce

Cooking Instructions:

1. Thinly slice the apple and remove the core. Add the graham cracker in the bottom of your air fryer.
2. Set the air fryer at 400°F and bake for 6 minutes. Halfway through the baking, flip the graham cracker, and continue backing.
3. After baking, remove the graham cracker and allow it to cool for a couple of minutes. Place 3-4 slices of apple on the graham cracker.
4. Top it with 1 teaspoon caramel sauce. Add the marshmallows in the air fryer basket. Set the temperature to 360°F and cook for 8 minutes.
5. Shake the air basket halfway through the cooking. Add the roasted marshmallows on top of the apple slices.
6. Again, place one graham cracker over it.
7. Serve topped with caramel sauce.

Nutritional Information:

Calories: 165, Total fat: 2.9g, Saturated fat: 0.4g, Cholesterol: 0mg, Sodium: 194mg, Total carbs: 33.9g, Dietary fiber: 2.2g, Total sugars: 14.6g, Protein: 2.2g, Calcium: 11mg, Potassium: 103mg

Air Fryer S'mores

Preparation time: 5 minutes

Cooking time: 5 minutes

Total time: 10 minutes

Servings: 4

Ingredients:

- 4 pieces of chocolate
- 4 marshmallows
- 4 whole graham crackers

Cooking Instructions:

1. Make 8 squares from the graham crackers. Cut the marshmallows in cross position using scissors.
2. Place the marshmallows on 4 Grahams square in cut side down position.
3. Set the air fryer at 390°F. Add the marshmallows in the air fryer basked facing upside. Cook for 5 minutes until it becomes golden brown.
4. After 5 minutes, transfer them to serving bowl. Add a chocolate piece and graham square on top of the toasted marshmallow.
5. Serve hot and enjoy!

Nutritional Information:

Calories: 7, Total fat: 0.2g, Saturated fat: 0.1g, Cholesterol: 0mg, Sodium: 7mg, Total carbs: 1.2g, Dietary fiber: 0.1g, Protein: 0.1g, Calcium: 1mg, Potassium: 1mg

French Toast Sticks

Preparation time: 5 minutes

Cooking time: 30 minutes

Total time: 35 minutes

Servings: 6

Ingredients:

- 6 thick slices of a white loaf.
- 3 tbsp. granulated sugar
- ½ tsp. vanilla extract
- ¼ tsp. kosher salt
- ¼ cup of maple syrup
- 2 large eggs
- ⅓ cup whole milk
- ⅓ cup heavy cream
- ¼ tsp. ground cinnamon

Cooking Instructions:

1. Cut the loaves into three pieces.
2. In a large bowl, whisk milk, eggs, cream, a pinch of salt, and vanilla.
3. Put bread and turn to coat all sides. Set the air fryer at 375°F.
4. Add the coated bread pieces into the air fryer basket without overlapping.
5. Start cooking for 8 minutes until it becomes golden brown.
6. Flip the breadsticks midway through the cooking. Drizzle maple syrup while serving.
7. Serve hot and enjoy!

Nutritional Information:

Calories: 113, Total fat: 4.6g, Saturated fat: 2.3g, Cholesterol: 73mg, Sodium: 130mg, Total carbs: 15.9g, Dietary fiber: 0.1g, Total sugars: 14.7g, Protein: 2.7g, Calcium: 38mg, Potassium: 74mg

Molten Lava Cake

Preparation time: 15 minutes

Cooking time: 13 minutes

Total time: 28 minutes

Servings: 4

Ingredients:

- 3½ ounces dark chocolate, chopped
- 3½ tbsp. Baker's Sugar
- 3½ ounces, unsalted butter 4 ramekins
- 1½ tbsp. flour, self-rising
- 2 eggs
- Cooking spray

Cooking Instructions:

1. Set the Air Fryer at 375°F and preheat.
2. Spray the ramekins with cooking spray and sprinkle some flour in the ramekins.
3. Add the butter and chocolate in a microwave oven for 3 minutes. Remove it from the microwave and stir until it turns into an even consistency.
4. In a medium bowl, beat the eggs and sugar until it turns frothy. Transfer melted chocolate into the beaten egg mixture.
5. Add flour and combine thoroughly using a spatula. Fill the ramekins ¾ and place in the air fryer baking tray for 10 minutes.
6. After 10 minutes, transfer it to a cooling rack to cool for a couple of minutes. Loosen the edges of the ramekins with a butter knife.
7. Flip the ramekins in the serving plate. Tap on the top side until the cake gets released from the ramekin.
8. Serve fresh and enjoy!

Nutritional Information:

Calories: 767, Total fat: 35.6g, Saturated fat: 23.8g, Cholesterol: 198mg, Sodium: 175mg, Total carbs: 65.4g, Dietary fiber: 3.7g, Total sugars: 56.7g, Protein: 44.2g, Calcium: 232mg, Potassium: 759mg

Cinnamon Rolls

Preparation time: 5 minutes

Cooking time: 25 minutes

Total time: 30 minutes

Servings: 6

Ingredients:

- 8 ounces tube crescent rolls, refrigerated 3 tablespoons melted butter.
- ⅓ cup brown sugar
- ¼ tsp. kosher salt
- ½ tsp. ground cinnamon
- ¼ cup all-purpose flour

For Making the Glaze:

- 1 tbsp. whole milk
- ½ cup powdered sugar
- 2 ounces cream cheese, kept in room temperature (soft)

Cooking Instructions:

Making the rolls:

1. In a medium bowl, mix together the sugar, butter, salt, and cinnamon until it becomes a smooth cream.
2. Spread a baking sheet at the bottom of the air fryer and brush some butter.
3. On your working table, spread some flour and spread the crescent rolls. Crimp the edges and fold into half.
4. Make a 9" x 7" rectangle. Spread the sugar-butter-cinnamon mixture over the dough by leaving some space towards the edge portion.
5. Roll up the dough from the long side and slice into 6 pieces. Place the pieces in the air fryer basket, keeping the cut side up. Do not overlap the rolls.
6. Set the air fryer at 350°F and cook for 10 minutes.

Making the glaze:

7. In a medium bowl, whisk together the milk, powdered sugar and cream cheese.
8. Drop the glaze over the warm rolls while serving.

Nutritional Information:

Calories: 292, Total fat: 11.7g, Saturated fat: 6.3g, Cholesterol: 27mg, Sodium: 372mg, Total carbs: 42g, Dietary fiber: 1g, Total sugars: 19.9g, Protein: 5.5g, Calcium: 89mg, Potassium: 86mg.

Crustless Cheesecake

Preparation time: 10 minutes

Cooking time: 10 minutes

Total time: 20 minutes

Servings: 2

Ingredients:

- 16 ounces cream cheese, kept in room temperature
- 2 tbsp. sour cream
- ½ tsp. lemon juice
- 1 tsp. vanilla extract
- 2 eggs
- ¾ sweetener, zero calorie

Cooking Instructions:

1. Set the air fryer at 350°F and start preheating.
2. In a medium bowl, combine together the sweetener, eggs, lemon juice, and vanilla in a blender until it becomes smooth.
3. Add cream cheese and sour cream to the blender. Continue blending until it becomes very smooth.
4. Transfer the batter into a 4" springform pan and place inside the air fryer.
5. Set the timer for 10 minutes and start baking. When the baking is over, allow it to cool for a couple of minutes.
6. Refrigerate the cheesecake for 3 hours before serving.
7. Serve and enjoy!

Nutritional Information:

Calories: 886, Total fat: 86g, Saturated fat: 52.8g, Cholesterol: 418mg, Sodium: 740mg, Total carbs: 7.7g, Dietary fiber: 0g, Total sugars: 1.6g, Protein: 23.1g, Calcium: 219mg, Potassium: 351mg

Fried Oreos

Preparation time: 10 minutes

Cooking time: 4 minutes

Total time: 14 minutes

Servings: 9

Ingredients:

- 1 tbsp. sugar powder
- ¼ tsp. ground cinnamon
- 1 crescent sheet roll
- 9 Oreo cookies

Cooking Instructions:

1. Spread the crescent sheet on your working table.
2. Cut the sheets into 9 equal squares. Then, carefully wrap each Oreos with the crescent sheets.
3. Set the air fryer to 0360°F and start preheating.
4. Add the cookies in the air fryer basket without overlapping. Cook the cookies for 4 minutes. Flip the cookies halfway through the cooking.
5. Sprinkle ground cinnamon and sugar powder of the cookies at the time of serving.
6. Serve hot and enjoy!

Nutritional Information:

Calories: 67, Total fat: 3g, Saturated fat: 1g, Carbs: 10g, Protein: 1g, Sodium: 80mg, Potassium: 26mg, Dietary fiber: 1g, Sugar: 5g, Calcium: 3mg

Vegan Beignets

Preparation time: 45 minutes

Cooking time: 15 minutes

Total time: 1 hour

Servings: 24

Ingredients:

For the baking blend:

- 1 tsp. organic corn starch
- 1 cup sweetener

For the proofing:

- 1½ tsp. active baking yeast
- 1 cup full-fat coconut milk
- 3 tbsp. powdered baking blend

For the dough:

- 2 tsp. vanilla
- 3 cups unbleached white flour + 2 tablespoons flour
- 2 tbsp. melted coconut oil
- 2 tbsp. aquafaba (the drained water from canned chickpeas)

Cooking Instructions:

1. Add the sweetener and cornstarch in an electric blender and blend until it becomes a smooth powder.

2. Heat the coconut oil and let it cool down. Add the oil into the mixer and add yeast and sugar.

3. Keep it in the mixer for 10 minutes until it begins to produce foam. Add vanilla and aquafaba. Give everything a good mix.

4. Start adding the flour cup by cup. Continue mixing until forms like a dough for about 3 minutes. Scoop the dough and make a ball with your hand.

5. In a medium bowl, add the ball and cover it with a clean dishtowel. Within 1 hour, the dough will start to rise.

6. Sprinkle some flour on your working station and place the dough on it. Make a rectangle shape in ⅓-inch thickness with the dough.

7. Cut the flat rectangle dough into 24 square pieces and let it stay there for 30 minutes. Set the air fryer to 390°F and start preheating.

8. Add the beignets in the air fryer basket without overlapping. Cook for 15 minutes. Flip the cookies midway through the cooking until it turns golden brown.

9. Before serving, top it with the powdered baking blend.

10. Serve immediately and enjoy!

Nutritional Information:

Calories: 102, Total fat: 3g, Saturated fat: 3g, Cholesterol: 0mg, Sodium: 2mg, Carbs: 15g, Dietary fiber: 1g, Sugar: 1g, Protein: 3g

Doughnuts

Preparation time: 10 minutes

Cooking time: 2 hours 30 minutes

Total time: 2 hours 40 minutes

Servings: 6

Ingredients:

For Making the Donuts:

- 2 cups all-purpose flour
- 4 tbsp. butter melted
- 1 egg, large
- 1 tsp. vanilla extract
- ½ cup milk
- 2¼ tsp. dry yeast ¼ cup + 1 teaspoon sugar.
- ½ tsp. salt Cooking spray

For Making the Vanilla Glaze:

- 1 cup powdered sugar
- ½ tsp. vanilla extract
- 2 ounces milk

For Making the Chocolate Glaze:

- ¼ cup cocoa powder, unsweetened
- 3 tbsp. milk
- ¾ cup powdered sugar

For Making the Cinnamon Sugar:

- 2 tbsp. melted butter
- 2 tbsp. ground cinnamon
- ½ cup granulated sugar

Cooking Instructions:

Making the Donuts:

1. In a microwave-safe bowl, add the milk and microwave it for 40 seconds until it gets lukewarm. Add 1 tsp. of sugar and stir to dissolve.

2. After that, drizzle yeast and wait for about 8 minutes until it becomes frothy.

3. In a medium bowl, whisk together the salt and flour. Spray another large bowl with some cooking oil.

4. Combine the remaining ¼ cup of sugar, egg, butter, and vanilla in the large bowl. Add the yeast mixture into it and mix well.

5. Add the dry ingredients while stirring until it becomes a rough dough. Spread some flour on the working table.

6. Transfer the rough dough on to it and knead until it becomes elastic. Continue working on it for 5 minutes.

7. Add 1 tsp. of flour at a time to maintain its elastic consistency. Make small balls with the dough and place it in an oiled bowl.

8. Cover the dough balls with a clean dish towel and allow it to rise. Within 1 hour, it will double its size.

9. Then, stake out each ball and place it on the floured working table. Press it and make a ½-inch rectangle.

10. Cut the rectangle dough into the doughnut shape using a doughnut cutter. Collect the scrap dough and knead to make more doughnuts.

11. Spread baking sheets in a tray and place the doughnuts onto it. Cover it with a dishtowel and wait for 1 hour to rise it again.

12. Spray some cooking oil onto the air fryer and place the doughnuts without overlapping. Set the temperature to 375°F.

13. Cook for 6 minutes until it becomes golden brown. After cooking, transfer it on a cooling rack. Follow the same procedure for the remaining doughnut.

14. Dredge the doughnut in the glaze and allow it to cool for 5 minutes before serving.

Making the Vanilla Glaze:

1. Combine milk, powdered sugar, and vanilla until it becomes smooth.

Making the Chocolate Glaze:

1. In a medium bowl, mix together the cocoa powder, powdered sugar, and milk until it becomes smooth.

Making the Cinnamon Sugar:

1. Whisk sugar and ground cinnamon in a shallow bowl. Slightly coat melted butter over the doughnuts and sprinkle sugar and cinnamon mix.

Nutritional Information:

Calories: 216, Total fat: 2.9g, Saturated fat: 1.3g, Cholesterol: 31mg, Sodium: 232mg, Total carbs: 39.8g, Dietary fiber: 4.2g, Total sugars: 2.9g, Protein: 9g, Calcium: 100mg, Potassium: 255mg

CPSIA information can be obtained
at www.ICGtesting.com
Printed in the USA
LVHW050026090223
738857LV00006B/57

9 781952 504969